JOHN L. STODDARD'S LECTURES

BERLIN   VIENNA

ST. PETERSBURG   MOSCOW

Norwood Press
J. S. Cushing & Co. — Berwick & Smith
Norwood, Mass., U.S.A.

Macdonald & Sons, Bookbinders, Boston

JOHN L. STODDARD'S LECTURES

ILLUSTRATED AND EMBELLISHED WITH VIEWS OF THE
WORLD'S FAMOUS PLACES AND PEOPLE, BEING
THE IDENTICAL DISCOURSES DELIVERED
DURING THE PAST EIGHTEEN
YEARS UNDER THE TITLE
OF THE STODDARD
LECTURES

COMPLETE IN TEN VOLUMES

VOL. VI

BOSTON
BALCH BROTHERS CO.
MDCCCXCIX

BERLIN

BERLIN

O NE July night, in 1870, when Louis Napoleon's declaration of war against Prussia had become known, the streets of Paris echoed to one wild exultant cry, voiced from ten thousand throats, as frenzied crowds surged down the Boulevards, applauding, cheering, and deliriously shouting, "To Berlin! To Berlin!" And yet the men who shouted thus, in expectation of an easy victory, never beheld Berlin except perhaps as prisoners. Their dreams of a renewal of the first Napoleon's conquests were rapidly and cruelly dispelled. Still, as events have proved, there was in this Parisian cry a wonderful significance. Thereafter "To Berlin," the city of the conquerors, was to pass the military prestige till then held by France. "To Berlin" were to flow in golden streams five thousand million francs, which bleeding France gave up in payment for her rashness.

PRINCE BISMARCK AND HIS DOGS.

"To Berlin" also came amazing honors; for, as the Prussian King, even in the historic palace of Versailles, had been proclaimed Emperor of United Germany, so, from the German victories in France, Berlin arose to be not only chief of Prussian towns, but the political centre of the empire. Since then the cry of Germans also has been "To Berlin," and her increase in population surpasses that of any capital in Europe, except London.

A CORNER IN BERLIN.

The rapid growth of many American cities can be readily understood because of the newness of the country and their extremely favorable situations; but Berlin has no harbor like the New York bay and no river like the Hudson, nor does it, like Chicago, lie upon the shore of a vast inland sea. Nevertheless, its future is apparently secure, not only as the seat of

THE HOUSE OF PARLIAMENT.

the Imperial Court and Parliament, the centre of German military art, and the possessor of a university with five thousand students and hundreds of professors, but, also, as a city of manufactures and a centre for a vast amount of commerce.

No one can understand the Fatherland, to-day, without a visit to this great metropolis. For Berlin is at once the brain and arm of that gigantic frame known as United Germany, and it is Berlin more than aught else which has transformed the Germany of peaceful legends and romantic ruins, into the greatest military power upon earth, — the Germany of blood and iron, of cannon and of conquest, of Bismarck and Von Moltke.

The tourist from the west enters Berlin at present by a path of steel, which renders the journey thither from the Rhine a trifling matter of a few hours. One's first arrival in a foreign city is at times annoying, but in Berlin the usual difficulties vanish at the start. However small his knowledge of the German tongue may be, he need not dread his first encounter with the Berlin hackmen. Nothing could be more admirably managed. Each traveler, as he leaves the train, is asked by an official if he desires a cab. No

A BIT OF BERLIN.

long reply is necessary. The simple words *Ja wohl* are quite sufficient; and, in response, the tourist receives a metal check bearing a number. Holding this in his hand, as if about to pay his lunch-bill in an American restaurant, he walks to the exterior of the station. Here are apparently neither carriages nor drivers, but only an obsequious porter who takes the check and reads its number. This number corresponds, however, to one which glistens on the hat of an attendant coachman, who, though unseen, is eagerly waiting to hear it called. As soon as this is done, a carriage whirls around the corner and approaches. It is the cab assigned by lot, and the delighted tourist is driven in it to his destination. None but Americans can fully comprehend the blessed calm that falls upon the traveler's soul in consequence of this arrangement. For when we recollect the mobs of hackmen at our stations who, like a certain character mentioned in the Bible, go about like roaring lions seeking whom they may devour, we ask ourselves if Germany does not furnish us, in this respect, a greatly needed lesson.

Put in good humor by this well-trained service, when I emerged from my hotel, a few hours after my arrival in Berlin, I turned at once to the historic portal, of which the Berlinese are justly proud, — the Brandenburg Gate.

It is in truth imposing, being some seventy feet in height
and two hundred in breadth, and perforated by five different
passageways, the central one being reserved for carriages of
royalty. "Observe," said my companion, an old resident of
Berlin, "observe that chariot on the summit. It has been
something of a traveler. When Napoleon in 1806 passed,
as a conqueror, under this arch, he ordered that its car of
Victory be sent to Paris to adorn one of his own triumphal
arches there; but after his downfall, the Prussians brought
it back with shouts of exultation, restored the Goddess of
Victory to her throne on the Brandenburg Gate, and, still
further to testify their joy and pride, named the fine square
on which she looks the 'Place of
Paris.'"

THE BRANDENBURG GATE.

Thus speaking, we had walked beneath the arch and gazed upon it from the other side. "Do not forget," remarked my friend, "that through these parallel arcades, and in the very direction in which we are now looking, triumphal entries into Berlin are always made. No matter at what station royal visitors alight, they are, if possible, conducted to this gate, so that their first impressions of Berlin may prove agreeable." Of all the grand displays, however, on which

HAMBURG RAILWAY STATION.

BELLE ALLIANCE PLATZ.

the old historic portal has looked down, the most inspiring occurred in 1871, when the old Emperor, the Crown Prince, Bismarck, and Von Moltke, together with many of the war-scarred veterans who had so recently beheld, as conquerors, the Arch of Triumph on the Champs Élysées, marched beneath this into their own loved capital, welcomed by thousands of admiring relatives and friends. Those who witnessed that great scene can hardly speak of it even now without a tremor in their voices, and their eyes filling with tears.

The Brandenburg Gate forms the commencement of Berlin's most celebrated street, — the Unter den Linden, or "Under the Lime Trees." The name suggests abundant

BERLIN.

foliage, and I was disappointed to find that many of the
lindens were scrawny, miserable trees, which furnished little
ornament or shade. The street itself, however, is a fine one,
— straight as an arrow, and a mile in length; and, at a distance of two hundred feet, imposing buildings rise on either
side. The Unter den Linden cannot for a moment be ranked
in brilliancy and beauty with either the Champs Élysées,

UNTER DEN LINDEN.

or the boulevards of Paris; yet from the number of palaces,
monuments, and statues which adorn this thoroughfare, the
boast of the Prussians is probably true, that no city in the
world presents so many notable structures, on a single street,
as does Berlin.

One of these buildings is the Berlin Armory, appropriately
erected in the very heart of the city; for Mars, the god of
war, seems the divinity most worshiped here, and this great
edifice might be called his temple, to such an extent is it
adorned with warlike statues and insignia. In this respect,

Berlin is preëminent. Most other German towns impress us
with a feeling of antiquity. In them historic buildings, venerable streets, or old cathedrals greet us at every turn. But
in Berlin all this is changed. One feels instinctively that
ancient monuments are no more to be looked for here than
in a camp. "Prussia," a witty Frenchman says, "was born
from a cannon-ball, like an eagle from an egg."

THE BRANDENBURG GATE, SEEN FROM THE UNTER DEN LINDEN.

The Prussian arsenal contains not only a wonderful collection of weapons, cannon, and armor of all ages and
nations, but also models of famous fortresses, and a great
number of standards taken from the enemy. Moreover, in
the story over these, as if to emphasize the fact that Prussia's glory rests on force of arms, are some superbly decorated halls containing bronze and marble statues of her kings

and heroes, as well as. historical paintings portraying such inspiring scenes as the "Proclamation of the German Empire at Versailles," "The Meeting of the Kaiser and Crown Prince at Königgrätz," and "The Capitulation of Sedan."

In the general character of its ornamentation Berlin is the most warlike of cities. No other capital in Europe has so many statues in its streets, yet almost every one portrays some military hero or some warlike deed. Thus, within a little distance of each other are the figures of Frederick the Great with his attendant generals, and the great Prussian leaders in the national uprising

THE ARMORY.

against Napoleon, — Blücher, York, Gneisenau, Bülow, and Scharnhorst. That of Blücher is particularly striking, and represents him bareheaded, standing on a prostrate cannon, and waving his sword, while apparently uttering his famous cry of "*Vorwärts.*"

Such statues make the Unter den Linden a kind of Triumphal Way and suggest courage, victory, and conquest. In time of peace they are impressive; in time of war they must be thoroughly inspiring. At every step the dullest cannot fail to comprehend that he is in a nation of warriors. Nowhere is this better exemplified than by the

groups of statuary on some of the Berlin bridges.   One, in
particular, personifies Prussia ; and without doubt the sculptor's idea was correct.   For what could be more characteristic
of the Prussian nation, under its present *régime*, than the
portrayal of a stalwart warrior teaching an ardent youth
the art of war?   Such, certainly, has been
the spirit of Prussia ever since her
humiliation by Napoleon, when
she resolved to profit by her
overthrow, and some day take
a terrible revenge.   At that
time, when a celebrated
Berlin teacher led his pu-
pils through the Bran-
denburg Gate, he would
always ask them, "Of what
are you thinking?"   If they
did not return a satisfac-
tory reply, he would
upbraid them with the
words: "You should
be remembering here

YOUTHFUL INSPIRATION.

that you are the children of the vanquished ; and that your
first resolve, as men, must be to march to Paris, and bring
back thence the car of Victory stolen from this gate by the
robber Napoleon."   It must be said that the counsel was
obeyed.

Another important edifice in Berlin is the War Academy,
which has a library of nearly a million volumes designed
exclusively to give army officers instruction in the art of
war.   But chief of all the fine memorials of war, which
Prussia's capital contains, is the imposing Monument of Victory erected near the Brandenburg Gate.   This splendid
work of art commemorates the three great wars of recent

times which have made Prussia what she is to-day. Its style
of decoration is unique. The column is divided into three
sections, one above the other, and into the surface of each
have been chiseled twenty parallel and perpendicular grooves.
These contain rows of Danish, French, and Austrian cannon, bound to the stone, apparently, by laurel wreaths of
gold. Moreover, towering far above these, and standing on
a capital formed of Prussian eagles, is a colossal statue
of Victory, which is itself nearly fifty feet in altitude and
one hundred and fifty feet above the pavement. The Emperor
William I., when he unveiled this figure at the dedication of
the column, on the third anniversary of the capitulation of
Sedan, must have experienced a proud satisfaction, as he beheld
the magnificent reliefs which decorate the pedestal of this
historic monument. For these, in forms that will defy the
touch of Time, portray the principal scenes connected with
the three campaigns, by means of which
the Prussian monarchy gained the exalted
position it now holds. One of the finest
of the reliefs represents a French general bringing to the Germans at Sedan
the letter of Napoleon III., announcing
his surrender; another recalls the triumphal entry of the Germans into
Paris; while a third por-
trays the memorable scene,
already mentioned, when
the victorious troops, headed
by the Kaiser, the Crown
Prince, Bismarck and Von
Moltke, reëntered Ber-
lin at the conclusion
of the Franco-Prussian
War.

A WARLIKE GROUP.

But Berlin's military air is not confined to buildings and statues. Platoons of soldiers in real flesh and blood frequently march along its streets, attended by admiring throngs. In fact, inspiring martial music is so common in Berlin, that the discouraged organ-grinders have been forced to emigrate to more peaceful lands. At every turn one sees a group of officers, their long mustaches twisted out like whip cords, their sabres clanking on the pavement.

It is part of discretion, if not of valor, for even ladies to give these sons of Mars a wide berth; since it seems to be derogatory to a Prussian officer's dignity to swerve a hair's breadth from his chosen course for any one who does not wear a uniform, and gallantry to ladies is not carried by German soldiers to the extent of stepping courteously aside to let them pass. Frequently in restaurants and theatres more soldiers can be counted than civilians; and we can, therefore, understand the lament of the German matron when she cried, "*Ach, du liebe Zeit!* See the effect of war upon our children. If we have handsome, well-made boys, they join the military; if we have girls, the military joins them."

Berlin has improved wonderfully in the last quarter of a century. The tourist who visited the Prussian capital about the time of the war with France would be delighted and surprised to-day at the amelioration of its avenues, the banishment of surface-drainings, the smoothness of its pavements,

THE COLUMN OF VICTORY.

THE UNTER DEN LINDEN, FACING THE STATUE OF FREDERICK.

the stateliness of its new buildings, and, above
all, the elegant residence-quarter which has
arisen near the Thiergarten, and in the
direction of the Potsdam station. Its
principal streets are worthy of admiration
now, as almost ideal city thoroughfares.
They are paved with asphalt, and
in the early morning are washed
thoroughly, a brigade of boys
invariably following up the water-
force with mops and sponges.
These boys are uniformed, and
work as systematically as if they
formed a section of the army.

A SOLDIER'S FAREWELL.

In fact, a kind of military discipline appears to govern every-
body in Berlin, high and low, rich and poor. Thus, if one
takes a cab to the theatre, the driver is obliged, a moment
before arriving, to stop and collect his fare, so that there
shall be no delay in the crowd about the entrance. Once there,
he merely leaves his passengers and drives immediately away.

The glory not alone of the Unter den Linden, but of all
Berlin, is the equestrian statue of
Frederick the Great, a work of the
famous sculptor Rauch. It represents
the King in his usual dress, including
his well-known military cloak and
old three-cornered hat; and so re-
markably life-like are his face and
attitude that one can easily imagine
him really seated upon his favorite
horse, reviewing silently the restless
crowd continually passing at his feet.

On close examination of this work
of art, my admiration was divided

FREDERICK THE GREAT.

between the figure of the King and the elaborate decoration
of the pedestal.   Perhaps the latter is the greater artistic
triumph; for on each of the four sides is an uninterrupted

A STREET SCENE IN BERLIN.

line of life-sized statues in bronze, some on horseback,
others on foot, each alleged to be an accurate likeness
of the hero or statesman whom it represents.   Some of
these figures are almost entirely distinct from their companions, forming as many separate subjects for examination,
and the entire group appears so animated, that one almost
expects to see it move along, — a splendid escort to that
king, who was at once a soldier, poet, and philosopher.

One day, as I was passing this monument, I found it
utilized in a way that would no doubt have horrified the
sculptor.   A dozen men and women were standing by the
railing, mournfully waving papers in the air, like shipwrecked
mariners showing signals of distress.   I soon discovered that
these poor people were petitioners, seeking to attract the
attention of the Emperor or Empress, if they should approach

the windows of the neighboring palace. It seems that this custom is allowed; for, after a time, I saw a soldier come out of the Kaiser's residence, collect the petitions, and carry them in for the imperial inspection. Close by this statue on the Unter den Linden stands a sombre, melancholy looking structure, apparently in want of a second story. It is the Guard House of the Royal Palace. Here soldiers always stand in readiness to quell the slightest insurrection; or, in default of any such excitement, to hurry out, fall into line, and present arms to any royal or distinguished personage who happens to be passing. Accordingly, the sentinels have not a moment's peace. They must not only keep a sharp lookout for all approaching dignitaries, but must salute every officer who comes in sight; and as the number of officers on this Berlin promenade is almost beyond computation, the arms of the poor sentries rise and fall with the precision of machinery.

Beyond the Guard House is a spacious square, which forms the other extremity of the Unter den Linden, a mile from the Brandenburg Gate. Here droshky drivers wait for "fares" with real Teutonic patience. Do not fear to approach them. Compared with other hackmen in the world, they are what the domesticated dog is to the wolf. We have already seen their wonderful subjection at the railroad station; and even on the street they are obliged to

assume a virtue, if they have it not. The rules restraining them are rigidly enforced. They dare not, therefore, overcharge, although their fares are low. A drive for less than a quarter of an hour costs fifteen cents in a second-class droshky, and twenty-five cents in a first-class cab, for one or two persons; and since Berlin is compact, a short drive will take the tourist from his hotel to almost any point

THE GUARD HOUSE.

of interest. Still further to protect the passenger from being overcharged, some modern Berlin cabs have an automatic machine on the back of the driver's seat, which, in accordance with the number of revolutions of the axle, indicates on a large dial the exact fare. There can be no dispute. Figures are not supposed to lie, even if coachmen do.

> "The Moving Finger writes; and, having writ,
> Moves on; nor all your Piety nor Wit
> Shall lure it back to cancel half a Line."

There are such vehicles in Berlin as third-class drosh-kies; but I never entered one of them, through fear of for-feiting my life insurance.

In strolling about Berlin, one soon discovers that, notwith-standing all its military power, the Government cannot wholly remedy the city's unfortunate situation. It lies in the midst of such a sandy plain that the Viennese call it jestingly the "sand-box of Germany," from the great clouds of dust which sometimes make its streets unbearable. Moreover, its low level has worse con-sequences than a sandy soil. The good old lady who thought it was owing to a kind act of Providence that rivers usually flowed beside important cities, must have be-lieved Berlin to be neglected by the gods; for the river Spree, which creeps on through the Prussian capi-tal, is a dull, languid stream, the odors of which cannot be surpassed,

THE CAFÉ BAUR.

save by the fumes rising from the canals connected with it.
Sometimes, when I have stood on one of Berlin's numerous
bridges in the summer months, I have been conscious of a
medley of rebellious smells, which all the gods of war could
not suppress.   Even the Berlinese acknowledge this defect;
and a comic paper recently described how a despairing lover,
wishing to commit suicide in a legal manner, accomplished

THE POLYTECHNIC SCHOOL, CHARLOTTENBURG.

his purpose by
merely hovering
for some hours
on the banks of
one of these pes-
tiferous canals.

A very promi-
nent building in
Berlin, and an-
other conspicuous
feature of the
Unter den Linden,
is the Royal Mu-
seum, founded by
Frederick William
III.   in   1824.
Fronting upon a
handsome   park,
adorned with statues, trees, and flowers, its site is superb,
and its dimensions are imposing.   A noble portico of Ionic
columns gives it an air of strength and majesty, while its
great height is shown by the four groups of statuary on
the roof, which, though colossal in themselves, appear diminutive on such a pedestal.   At the foot of the broad staircase
leading to this museum is an enormous basin of polished
granite, sixty-six feet in circumference and weighing seventy-
five tons, yet hewn from a single granite boulder, left by some

THE RIVER SPREE.

southward moving glacier, countless centuries ago, within
thirty miles of the site of the future Berlin. But this does
not appear extraordinary to a native of Berlin. It seems to
him quite natural that Providence should have foreordained
the leaving of that boulder, just where it fell, to decorate
the future Prus-
sian capital. *"Est
ist colossal,"* they
say of it, *"ganz
colossal" ;* which
is, indeed, the
phrase most often
heard from the
Berlinese,   as,
flushed with pride
and   satisfaction,
they describe the
buildings, monu-
ments, and pop-
ulation of their
city.

THE ARSENAL AND HALL OF FAME.

Every tourist
who stands before
the steps leading to this museum observes with admiration
the groups of statuary in bronze on either side. He might
expect that, at least, before a temple of the fine arts, some
peaceful statues would be placed; but this the warlike predi-
lections of the Berlinese forbid. One of these groups is the
famous work called the Lion Killer. It is evident that the
king of beasts has received a mortal wound, for a broken
spear-shaft has been buried in his side ; yet, even in the agony
of death, he has driven his claws into the side of the poor
horse, which rears in terror and in pain. Meantime the
conqueror, bestriding his unbridled steed with perfect ease,

adjusts his aim with a composure and consummate skill which indicate the issue of the combat. We are sure that in a moment more the monster will lie prostrate at his feet. Even more striking than this group is its companion on the other side of the staircase. Here the contending warrior is an Amazon. With her the conflict has become more desperate; for a powerful tiger, still unwounded, has leaped directly on her horse, driving both teeth and claws into the neck and breast of the poor beast, whose fear is admirably shown in his drooping ears and the wild movement of his eye, just visible above the tiger's head. This combat seems so doubtful, that

LION KILLER.

I could hardly contemplate it without a quicker beating of my heart, and an impatient wish that this unyielding, interlocked embrace might be relaxed and victory prevail for one side or the other.

The art-treasures in the Royal Museum are neither so numerous nor so valuable as those in several other European collections, because Berlin is young; and, when Frederick the Great began to purchase for his capital the masterpieces of the past, comparatively few could be obtained. Nevertheless, the selections have been made

AMAZON.

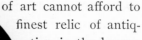

so carefully that lovers of art cannot afford to miss them. The finest relic of antiquity in the collection is the bronze statue known as "The Praying Boy," which is possibly a work of the school of Lysippus, dating from the fourth century before Christ. It was found in the bed of the Tiber, and, after undergoing partial restoration, was bought by Frederick the Great for about ten thousand dollars. To the Royal Museum has been added a noble edifice called the "New Museum," which is particularly rich in Egyptian relics, and casts of mediæval and modern sculpture. Its most attractive feature, however, is the series of magnificent frescos

HEAD OF
PRAYING BOY.

CRUSADERS AT JERUSALEM.

ROYAL MUSEUM.

by Kaulbach which adorn the grand staircase. This gigantic
work, to which the artist devoted nineteen years of toil, illus-
trates the history and development of the race from the heroic
age of Homer, through the destruction of Jerusalem, and
the exploits of the Crusaders, to the time of the Reforma-
tion. Although modern works these mural paintings would
certainly have been admired by the
greatest masters of antiquity, and are

ROYAL THEATRE.

themselves enough to give Berlin a high position in the realm of the fine arts.

Almost directly opposite the museum stands the Royal Opera House, erected by that ardent lover of music Frederick the Great, who tried in every way to make Grand Opera successful in his capital. It must be said that the frail plant, fostered by the Prussian King, has grown and flourished wonderfully. I do not know a city where permanent opera is better patronized. Often, when no remarkable attraction has been advertised, I have been unable to find a good seat in the house. How thoroughly the Germans seem to enjoy an operatic performance! In other portions of the world people too frequently attend the opera merely to see and to be seen. In Germany, however, the music in itself attracts them. Moreover, the Germans are most sensible in respect to their attendance at the opera and theatre. Recognizing the educational benefit to be derived from good music and fine dramatic performances, the Government gives financial aid to the best theatres in all large cities of the empire, so that a high standard of dramatic excellence may be maintained. The officers of the Prussian army are obliged to go, a certain number

STATUE OF FREDERICK III.

of times every month, to carefully selected places of amusement, as an aid to culture and refinement. The citizens themselves are so fond of operatic and dramatic performances
that they wish to attend more frequently than they could
possibly do, if such attendance always necessitated the keeping of late hours. Accordingly, even in Berlin, the time for
beginning the performance is often half-past six or seven

KROLL'S THEATRE.

o'clock, so that by ten the opera is over. The prices for
these entertainments are very reasonable. Seventy-five cents
will secure one of the best seats in many of the leading
theatres in Germany, and
tickets for the famous
Philharmonic concerts
in Berlin cost from ten
to twenty cents each.
In German theatres, also,
an admirable rule re-
quires the removal of
hats and bonnets. The
result of all this is an
audience which does not

ENTRANCE TO KROLL'S.

spend much thought on dress, but assembles for the enjoyment of the piece performed. The attention of the listeners
is, therefore, remarkable, and no applause is heard until
an act is finished. I greatly admire the respect that
Germans pay to music. Even in a concert-restaurant,
where hundreds of men and women are partaking of refreshments, the moment that the first strains of the orchestra are heard, the sound   of voices
and the clatter of dishes   cease,
and the great hall is
absolutely still until
the musical selec-
tion is complet-
ed. Then con-
versation, laugh-

FLORA IN CHARLOTTENBURG,
EXTERIOR.

ter, and lunch
begin again, to
continue until
another strain of
music once more
hushes all to
silence.

FLORA, INTERIOR.

Berlin is by
no means limited to imposing theatres. Some are quite
simple in appearance, and have connected with them
attractive gardens, which offer further recreation to their
patrons in avenues of trees, lighted with colored lamps

and jets of gas arranged in fanciful designs; while here and there is a pretty arbor, provided, of course, with a table and chairs; for, to be really happy, the Germans must, on public occasions, eat and drink.
The theatres, therefore, have their restaurants, which, when the curtain falls, are instantly invaded; and between every act the gardens become suddenly alive with thirsty people. One object then fills every soul with

KING S THEATRE.

longing. It is the characteristic, the inevitable beer-mug. Skilled hands have previously strewn upon the tables countless *steins* of beer; and at the sight of them a roar of voices fills the air, a clash of clinking mugs goes up to heaven, a thousand eager arms are raised, a thousand bearded mouths expand; a moment's silence then ensues; then crash! down go the beer-mugs on the quivering tables, drained of their contents once and yet again, ere the loud bell calls the invigorated wanderers in to see the curtain rise for another act.

In the basement of the Berlin City Hall there is an enormous restaurant, three hundred feet in length, and comfortably, even luxuriously,

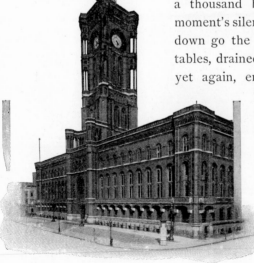

CITY HALL.

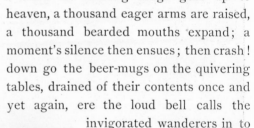

ROYAL UNIVERSITY.

furnished. Thus, while eloquence is flowing in the halls above, Rhine wine and beer are flowing in the vaults below. It has been calculated that two million glasses of beer are consumed in Berlin every day, or more than one glass for every man, woman, and child in the city. Yet little intoxication is seen here, for there are very few low saloons where ardent spirits are for sale. Occasionally, one finds in Germany "American Bars," where every kind of fancy drink known in the United States is advertised to be made, if called for; but these are little patronized, save by a few American travelers. Compared with German restaurants they seem unsocial; for, as a rule, an American

STATUE OF ELECTOR.

drinks standing at the bar, being in too much haste to seat himself and sip the beverage while listening to fine music, or reading thoughtfully his evening paper.

Among the equestrian statues on the Unter den Linden is the colossal figure of the Grand Elector, one of those magnates who, many years ago, possessed the power of choosing monarchs for the Prussian people. Times have changed greatly since his day, and Berlin has so altered with them that, if the Grand Elector could return to life, I fancy he

would stand as motionless as this statue, in dumb amazement at the improvements which have taken place.   He
would find, it is true, the Royal Palace confronting him
comparatively unaltered; but that is the only antique monument of importance which Berlin can claim, and even that,
in its present form, has seen scarcely two centuries.

This city residence of the present Kaiser is a building
of gigantic size, a kind of mountain faced with stucco.
Frederick the Great was born within its walls; but for many
years or until the accession of the present sovereign, it was not
used as an imperial abode.   Old Emperor William always
preferred the modest house built for him when a newly
married prince, and his son Frederick, had he lived, would
doubtless have followed his example.   But since this has been
always used for State receptions, Court ceremonies, festivals,
and royal weddings, it is revered by the Germans on account
of its participation in the great events connected with the
nation's history.   On entering the courtyard of this massive
edifice, I was amused to see another proof of the warlike
tastes of the Berlinese.   *Toujours la guerre!*   For here, im-
mortalized in bronze, is St.
George fighting with the
dragon.   A myth, of
course; yet not un-
suited to the

PALACE WITH WATER FRONT.

place, for this old palace has connected with it a number of mysterious legends which, by the common people, used to be accepted as undoubted facts. Such, for example, is the story of the White Lady, whose spectral figure is believed to haunt this castle, and frequently to walk unseen, though not unheard, through its seven hundred rooms. On rare occasions, however, it is said to be visible; and then the ghostly presence, it is thought, portends some great misfortune to the royal family. The phantom is supposed to be a German countess, Agnes of Orlamünde, who, centuries ago, with mediæval frankness offered her hand in marriage to a member of the royal house. The Prince replied that two pairs of eyes formed the sole obstacle to their union, alluding to his aged parents,

COURTYARD TO PALACE.

who would not give their consent to the nuptials. The countess, however, fancied that he referred to her two children by a former marriage, and caused them to be put to death. Yet, when she told her lover of the frightful crime, perpetrated for his sake, he cast her off in horror, and she committed suicide. Her spirit found no rest, however, and is doomed to haunt the royal household as a messenger of woe. We feel inclined to laugh at such a superstition, yet a belief in the White Lady, or at least a fear of her, actually caused the death of the grandfather of Frederick the Great. One day, as he was seated in this palace, his insane wife, who had escaped from her attendants, came rushing toward him, and sprang directly through the large glass door of the conservatory. Startled by the terrific crash, the old King turned around and saw advancing, apparently to attack him, a female clothed in white, waving her bleeding hands and uttering fearful cries. Believing that he saw in her the traditional ghost of the palace, the King fell senseless to the floor, and never recovered from the shock. His grandson Frederick was then fourteen months old.

BALL-ROOM.

The tourist cannot view this royal residence without some inconvenience; for, before he is allowed to take a step in its magnificent apartments, he is obliged to thrust his feet into enormous woolen slippers, so that his boots may not deface the exquisitely polished floors. Nothing is more ridiculous than to behold a group of travelers shuffling through a palace in this fashion; for these gigantic moccasins were modeled, apparently, not from the human foot, but after a canal boat on the river Spree. It is practically impossible to lift one's feet in them, and I have seen ladies and gentlemen helplessly staring at these pedal mastodons, or sliding recklessly about, like learners in the art of skating; while, since there are no small sizes, to see a wretched child trying to keep his balance in these number eighty-five foot-coverings, is enough to provoke screams of laughter.

The most magnificent apartment of the Royal Palace is its famous White Hall. This is of imposing size, and beautifully adorned with marble statues, elegant mirrors, bronze balconies, and crystal chandeliers, the total cost of which is estimated at more than a hundred thousand dollars. It has been used for many important ceremonies; and here the Prince of Wales, the Shah of Persia, the Tsar, and the King of Italy have been entertained. Here, too, the German Emperor always receives the members of Parliament at the opening of their session, when, standing beneath a gorgeous canopy, he delivers to them the imperial address.

WHITE HALL.

To examine the seven hundred apartments of this palace would be, of course, a hopeless task; but there is one, at least, which the tourist should not pass unnoticed. It is the

THRONE ROOM.

Throne Room. The decorations of this hall are extremely elegant; and beneath a gilded canopy and outlined against a background of velvet, studded with golden crowns, are the chairs of the Emperor and Empress. Blue was for many years the favorite color at festivals in this apartment, for of that tint old Emperor William was particularly fond. I do not know whether the present sovereign, his grandson, has the same taste; but, if so, it is probable that many ladies of the Prussian Court wear blue in an attempt to attract his attention. That this was done in flattery to the old Kaiser is no secret. In fact, all sorts of humorous stories have been told of this peculiarity of William I. Thus, a comic paper of Munich once declared that he chose a certain individual for his private secretary, simply because he wore blue spectacles.

THRONE.

During an earlier visit to Berlin, I saw in this Throne
Room, instead of the two royal chairs, the solid silver throne
presented to the Emperor by some officers of his army.
A famous German artist once begged permission to paint
a court ceremony in this apartment. He was told that he
might do so, provided the Emperor could see the prelimi-
nary sketch. The artist consented, and the plan was finally
submitted to the Kaiser for inspection. His Majesty was represented, seated on the throne, beside which stood the Crown
Prince with one
foot on the first
step. The bluff old
Kaiser frowned,
and, seizing a
pencil, quickly
changed the posi-
tion of his son,
so as to bring
both feet together
on the floor.
Then he returned
the sketch to the
painter with these
laconic words,
written beneath
the figure of

ROYAL SIDEBOARD.

"Our Fritz," *Noch nicht*, not yet! Opposite the throne,
on the other side of the apartment, stands what is claimed
to be the most magnificent sideboard in the world. To
the full height of the room, it is entirely covered with
antique gold and silver plate of the most elaborate description, as though the legendary Midas had been there to
transform every dish into gold. Moreover, in the foreground, and at the base of all this splendor, is a magnificently

decorated beer-mug, several feet in height, capacious enough to satisfy the wants of the entire royal family.

The presence of this flagon is not altogether inappropriate; for, firmly as the Kaiser is seated on the throne, the sovereign to whom the Germans pay absolute allegiance is old Gambrinus, king of beer. The father of Frederick the Great

DINING-ROOM.

advised his subjects to drink beer, which strengthened the body, rather than wine, which stole away the brains; and the Germans of to-day have this significant proverb: " He who is not strong before twenty, handsome before thirty, wise before forty, and rich before fifty, on such a man even beer is altogether lost."

NATIONAL GALLERY.

Not far from the Royal Castle is another structure, which, though much smaller and plainer in appearance, has for the tourist far greater interest. It was formerly the residence of old Kaiser William. Its situation is more imposing than the edifice itself, for it occupies a prominent position on the

OLD EMPEROR WILLIAM'S PALACE.

Unter den Linden, in close proximity to the armory and the museum, while the magnificent statue of Frederick the Great stands directly in front of it. I was surprised, as I suppose every visitor is, to find the exterior of this palace so unpretentious. Compared with other homes of royalty in Europe, such as the Winter Palace at St. Petersburg, or the Palace at Madrid, it appears insignificant. It is merely a plain, substantial house of stuccoed brick. A stranger might walk by, and fancy it the home of some private individual, unless the sentries at the door and the imperial eagles on the roof betrayed its ownership. The corner windows of this palace, on the ground floor, were those of the old Emperor's study; and every day at a quarter before one o'clock, when the troops marched past to take their station at the neighboring Guard House, one could almost invariably

see, at the window fronting on the Unter den Linden, the aged Kaiser and his favorite great-grandchild, returning the salutations of the soldiers and populace. This ceremony had for the child an unusual significance ; for it is the custom of every Prussian prince at his tenth year to become a lieutenant in the army. This daily greeting of his soldiers William I. maintained to the last days of his life, yet he would never present himself at the window save in military attire. In fact, when dressed, he was never

AT THE KAISER'S WINDOW.

without his uniform. In the privacy of his study he would, occasionally, loosen and throw back his coat, but at the sound of fife or drum he would always button it again, and

stand thus till the troops had passed. On being asked once why he took such pains to fasten every button, he replied : " I wish to set .a suitable example; for, let me tell you, it is the one clasp left unbuttoned that is the ruin of an army."

A PARADE IN THE UNTER DEN LINDEN.

Since the Emperor's death his home has been transformed into a kind of museum (one might almost say a

OLD KAISER WILLIAM.

shrine), devoted to memo-
rials of William and his
wife Augusta.   It is freely
open to the public at certain hours every day, and
it is interesting to observe
the love and reverence
evinced by the old Kaiser's
subjects, as they behold
his table, chair, personal
ornaments, and articles of
clothing, as well as the magnificent collection of presents bestowed upon him at
different epochs in his reign,

particularly on the occasion of his golden wedding.   Yet,
while these gifts are wonderfully rich and beautiful, the

apartments of the Emperor
are extremely plain.   In
his bedroom, for example,
I found the royal couch
to have been a simple iron
cot, — a relic and reminder
of his military life.   His
antechamber also was sim-
ply furnished, and bore no
trace of regal luxury.   Some
ordinary paintings and a
few engravings hung upon
the walls, and a sheaf of
battle-flags stood stiffly by
the door; but sculptured

THE EMPRESS AUGUSTA.

ornaments were rare, except, indeed, a little marble bust of Bismarck, standing without a rival on the centre table. A wonderfully impressive place to me is such a royal ante-room as this, when I reflect on all the thousands who have waited here at some great crisis in their lives, their fortunes staked, perhaps, on the result of the approaching interview, and destined probably, an hour later, to leave this room, their faces radiant with happiness or hopeless from disas-trous failure. On entering the private study of the Emperor, I could have easily supposed myself to be in an artist's studio; for the ottomans and tables are covered with portraits, pho-tographs, and medallions. There is, too, a confusion on the desk that makes every literary man immediately feel at home. Few writers are, however, favored with such beautiful table ornaments as those which here surrounded William I.

THE KAISER'S ANTECHAMBER.

I noticed that several pen-racks, clocks, thermom-eters, and paper-weights were made of malachite or lapis-lazuli, souve-nirs doubtless of a visit to St. Petersburg. But, as if such orna-ments were not sufficiently war-like, his inkstand was made from half of a cannon-ball, some of his penholders had been manufactured out of splintered Uhlan lances, and a couple of paper-weights were fashioned from the

hoofs of horses killed in battle. I observed, also, a bust of
Frederick the Great, and an equestrian statue of the Emperor's

THE KAISER'S STUDY.

father; while, opposite them, the sculptured face of his good
wife Augusta looked down with tranquillity, perhaps not quite
true to life, upon the wild disorder of the table.

During the reign of William I., the flags of the regiment
on duty at Berlin were kept in this palace. Accordingly,
whenever the guard assembled for review, the color-bearers
used to enter the royal residence to secure their standards,
which the Emperor frequently presented to them with his
own hands. I noticed hanging by the window in the Kaiser's

study, a calendar composed of three hundred and sixty-five
pages, each of which bore the date of the day of the month,
together with a verse from the Bible or a literary quota-
tion.   Below these were printed the chief events that had
occurred during the Kaiser's reign, including battles, victories,
births, deaths, travels, receptions, and sicknesses.   These,
in the life of as old a man as William I., were very
numerous, and morning after morning must have brought

IN THE EMPEROR'S PALACE.

a number of im-
portant anniver-
saries forcibly to
his attention.
Moreover, to in-
crease their value,
the Emperor was
in the habit of
writing on these
leaflets any re-
marks which he
desired to add to
the   collection,
and these would
duly appear in
their places on the
calendar of the
following year.

The Jewish Synagogue, in Berlin, is a magnificent structure, which can seat nearly five thousand people, and cost
about one and a half million dollars.   Its Moorish ara-
besques and arches, and the resplendent stained glass in
its dome and windows, give to the building an impression
of Oriental wealth and luxury that I have never seen in
other sanctuaries, save a few in Russia.   That this imposing Israelitish temple is, in its architectural beauty

EMPEROR WILLIAM I.

and the quality of its music, superior to any Christian church in the city, is a fact of great significance. The Hebrew element in Berlin, which numbers about seventy thousand souls, is very strong and influential. In spite of years of persecution and unjust oppression, the Jews to-day are among the foremost, not merely in commercial circles, but also in the ranks of doctors, journalists, and lawyers. Most of the Berlin newspapers are wholly, or in part, controlled by them; and the leader of the liberal party and the ablest debater in the Reichstag for years was the Hebrew Lasker. No doubt this is partly due to the fact that more than half the Jewish children in Berlin receive a liberal education, while only about one-fifth of the children of

THE JEWISH SYNAGOGUE.

other religions enjoy as good advantages. Yet, only half a century ago, no Berlin Jew could marry without special permission from the King. Frederick the Great took advantage of this law, after he had purchased the porcelain manufactory at Berlin, by insisting that every Hebrew couple should buy a certain amount of porcelain, the quantity to be purchased being specified on the margin of the marriage certificate.

One of the most delightful features of Berlin is the Thiergarten, a densely wooded and attractive park; beginning at the Brandenburg Gate and presenting thence, for two miles, a charming maze of drives and shaded walks, adorned with flowers and statues.

A portion of this park is devoted to a Zoölogical Garden, which must certainly rank among the largest, finest, and best managed in the world. Like most such gardens in Germany, it is owned and controlled by a stock company, and of late years has paid large dividends. It covers ninety acres of land, tastefully arranged, and on pleasant afternoons it is thronged with people. Whole families here spend hours at a time; the women with their fancy work, the children with their toys, — listening meantime to the music of one orchestra and sometimes that of two. In the latter case, one band will take up a selection the moment the other has concluded, so that the music is continuous.

AN AVENUE IN THE THIERGARTEN.

It is possible that the Germans enjoy and make use of outdoor life in summer more than Americans, because of the delightful contrast which the long summer days of northern Europe present to the short, gloomy days of winter

in that latitude. Berlin is really as far north as Labrador, and in the winter most of the daylight is restricted to the hours between eight in the morning and four in the afternoon. School children, therefore, in midwinter must breakfast by lamplight, and go forth to school while it is still

SCENERY IN THE THIERGARTEN.

dark. In summer, however, the days are correspondingly long, and the hours of sunshine and the lingering northern twilight are thoroughly appreciated.

The little stream that flows through the Thiergarten encircles several diminutive islands, the prettiest of which is called "Luisen-Insel," after the beloved and beautiful Queen Louisa of Prussia. It is appropriate that, perfectly mirrored in the stream beside this island, should stand the marble statue of her husband, Frederick William III.; for it was by his order, and to please his wife, that this section of the Thiergarten was transformed from a wilderness into a charming park. It is in many ways a very suggestive monument,

for it portrays the sovereign during whose reign Prussia received
her terrible humiliation from Napoleon; but while the Germans
are reminded by it of the
shame and suffering which
that monarch and his consort
endured after Napoleon's
victory at Jena, it also calls
to mind the complete retalia-
tion effected by their son, the
late Kaiser William.   On this
Luisen-Insel, and in close proximity to the figure of her husband,
stands a beautiful statue of Queen

QUEEN LOUISA.

Louisa, near which is the elegant vase sculptured by Schadow,
with its brief but eloquent inscription, "To the returning
Queen."   This, too, is a memorial of the
dark days of Prussian history; for it was
erected to welcome Queen Louisa,
when the retirement of the French
from Berlin made possible the return
of the royal family to the capital.

The Germans excel in repre-
sentations of their favorite Queen,
and the likeness to Louisa in this
statue is said to be remarkable.
Her noble, womanly nature is depicted in the face; the robe about
her graceful form seems satin in its
softened finish; while from her
shoulders falls a delicate lace mantle,
marvelously chiseled.   It is said that the

STATUE OF FREDERICK WILLIAM III.   late Emperor William, who adored his mother, would often halt before this figure in mute admiration. Nor is it strange; for what pathetic incidents of his childhood must have recurred to him, as he looked upon this beautiful memorial! One of these occurred after the defeat of Jena, when little William was but ten years old. Berlin was then occupied by the French, Prussia was panic-stricken, and Queen Louisa was fleeing with her children toward the frontier of Poland. Suddenly the carriage containing them broke down; and the unhappy Queen seated herself among her little ones beside the road, several miles distant from the nearest town. The youngest children cried from hunger (for in the haste of their departure, all food had been forgotten), and at the sight of their suffering the Queen wept bitterly. However, a wheat-field was close at hand, and she sent William into it to gather the blue corn-flowers which grew luxuriantly there. With these she made wreaths for their little heads, and thus beguiled the weary time until they could renew their journey. The Emperor never forgot that incident, and the blue corn-flowers of the wheat-field were always those which he most dearly loved. In fact, a vase filled with these flowers usually stood upon his study table, since he protested that, without the inspiration of their beauty and of the memories they awakened, he could not do his work well. Accordingly, corn-flowers were specially cultivated for this vase all the year round in a conservatory at Potsdam.

QUEEN LOUISA AND WILLIAM.

To those who admire and revere the memory of Queen Louisa, no excursion in the vicinity of Berlin is more interesting than to the extremity of the Thiergarten, where they may visit the palace of Charlottenburg, the favorite residence of Frederick

IN THE PARK AT CHARLOTTENBURG.

William III. and his beloved wife. It is not strange that the Prussians look upon the mother of old Emperor William as a kind of patron saint. Her death is believed to have been hastened by the terrible disasters brought upon her country by Napoleon, and hence her memory is cherished as that of a martyr to the cause of patriotism. When the King, her husband, died, many years after her decease, it was found that he had always worn her portrait on his breast; and in a similar way it may be said that her image is enshrined in every Prussian heart, like that of Washington in the hearts of millions of Americans, or that of Jeanne d'Arc in the affections of the French.

The penalty that Prussia

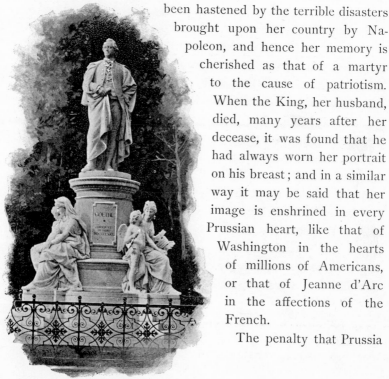

STATUE OF GOETHE.

paid for joining the coalition against Napoleon had, indeed, been terrible ; for by the treaty of Tilsit Frederick William III. was obliged to give up half of his kingdom, to reduce his army to forty-two thousand men, and to pay a war indemnity of more than one hundred million dollars, besides recognizing all the new kingdoms which Napoleon had established for himself and his brothers. To help the nation pay this enormous sum, the King and Queen sacrificed their own money and jewels, and lived in the simplest manner. Louisa retained one necklace of pearls, but of this she said sadly: " I allow myself to keep them ; for in Germany pearls signify tears, and they can well serve me for ornaments." Three years after the promulgation of the treaty of Tilsit Queen Louisa was dead.

One of the most pathetic utterances that ever fell from royal lips, was spoken by Frederick William III., when the physicians announced to him the probable death of his idolized wife. " Alas ! " exclaimed the unhappy sovereign, whose life had been for years a constant series of misfortunes, "if she were not mine, she might recover." The death of this beautiful and noble woman was attended with excruciating suffering. Her last words, uttered five minutes before her release, were, " Lord Jesus, make it short."

The most retired portion of the park, adjoining the palace of Charlottenburg, had been for Queen Louisa a favorite place of quiet recreation with her hus-

QUEEN LOUISA'S MONUMENT.

band and children. The spot seemed, therefore, sacred to
her memory, and here her remains were laid to rest in
a beautiful marble mausoleum, erected by order of the King.
Here also he, in his turn, was buried. For many years this
royal sepulchre held merely the remains of Frederick William III. and his wife; but the present Emperor has caused
it to be enlarged, and now it also contains the bodies of his
grandparents, —
William I. and
his wife Augusta.

THE LION'S BRIDGE IN THE THIERGARTEN.

Tombs of roy-
alty are numer-
ous in Europe, but
few can be com-
pared with that
of Charlottenburg
for beauty and
solemnity. The
walls and floors
are of polished
marble, upon
which falls a deli-
cately colored

light from stained glass windows in the roof; while, in the
centre, upon exquisitely sculptured couches, are the recumbent
figures of the royal dead. There is a beautiful repose about
these statues. With folded hands they seem to lie, not in
death, but

> " Like one who wraps the drapery of his couch about him,
>   And lies down to pleasant dreams."

Hither, as to a hallowed shrine, every year, on the anniversary of Queen Louisa's death, the members of the imperial family come to lay a floral tribute on her grave; and

THE HOTEL KAISERHOFF.

the same cere-
mony takes place
on the anniver-
saries of the
deaths of the old
Emperor and
Empress. It is
eminently fitting
that William I.
should be buried
here; for there
are no traits in his
character more
beautiful than his
adoration of, and
devotion to, his

THE MAUSOLEUM.

mother; and there are few events more touching than the
visits that he made to this, her tomb, before and after the

THE INTERIOR OF THE MAUSOLEUM.

war with France;
one, as it were,
to invoke her
blessing upon the
coming conflict;
the other, when
flushed with vic-
tory, to lay his
laurels at her feet.
One naturally
calls to mind, in
this consecrated
spot, the beautiful
stanzas of Mrs.
Hemans, descrip-
tive of the place:

" It stands where northern willows weep,
　A temple fair and lone;
Soft shadows o'er the marble sweep,
　From cypress branches thrown.

　　*　　*　　*　　*　　*　　*

And what within is richly shrined?
　A sculptured woman's form;
Lovely, in perfect rest reclined,
　As one beyond the storm;
Yet not in death, but slumber, lies
The solemn sweetness of those eyes.

　　*　　*　　*　　*　　*　　*

She slumbered, — but it came, it came;
　Her land's redeeming hour,
With the glad shout and signal flame
　Set on from tower to tower.
Fast through the realm a spirit moved,
'T was hers, the lofty and the loved!

Then was her name a note that rung
　To rouse bold hearts from sleep;
Her memory, as a banner flung
　Forth by the Baltic deep;
Her grief, a bitter vial poured
To sanctify the avenger's sword.

And the crowned eagle spread again
　Her pinion to the sun;
And the strong land shook off its chain;
　So was the triumph won!
But woe for earth, where sorrow's tone
Still blends with victory's, — *She* was gone."

" LOVELY, IN PERFECT REST RECLINED."

THE EMPEROR WILLIAM MEMORIAL CHURCH.

A few miles from Berlin is a fine château, which was frequently occupied by old Emperor William in summer. It is the Palace of Babelsberg. In its retirement and beautiful tranquillity it is, apparently, the very place for one engaged in literary pursuits; yet, as every one knows, William I. was no scholar. He had not even literary tastes. After his death a gentleman visited his palace in Berlin, and had the curi-

THE CHÂTEAU AT BABELSBERG.

osity to see what books had adorned the Kaiser's library and table. Without exception, they were all military handbooks. Of literature, properly so called, he did not find a single specimen. In this respect, what a contrast existed between the late Emperor and Frederick the Great, who, though a most successful soldier, had nevertheless his charming rooms at Sans Souci filled with the choicest books from every land! The bedroom of William I., at Babelsberg, was simply furnished. I noticed that the principal table ornaments were silver candlesticks, for the Kaiser always preferred wax candles to gas in his sleeping-room. As for the bed, despite its handsome canopy, I observed that the old German style was still maintained; that is to say, a narrow couch upon which balances a feather-bed in place of clothes. Without doubt there are persons who can sleep well on German beds thus made, and seemingly the Emperor could do so; but how they accomplish it, is to me a marvel. In all other parts of the world with which I am acquainted, a bed is — a bed. Thus, an English bed, a Spanish bed, a French, American, or Italian bed is a couch with a mattress, more or less hard, and with clothes that can be tucked in at the foot and sides. But in the Fatherland, an old-style bed compels you to lie on a space not much wider than that of a coffin, beneath a bag of feathers called a *decke*, and to remain there motionless, without the slightest toss or turn. Otherwise

THE TEA-ROOM.

THE LIBRARY.

the feather-bed will roll off on the floor, leaving your body exposed to sciatic rheumatism, and your mind in a condition which can be mildly described as that of nervous irritability. What wonder, then, that Coleridge, when traveling in the Fatherland, declared that rather than sleep in one of those German beds, he preferred to imitate the American Indian and carry his blanket around with him?

The most interesting excursion to be made in the vicinity of Berlin is to the Prussian Versailles,—Potsdam, with its

THE DINING-ROOM.

THE PARK OF SANS SOUCI.

historic palaces, including Sans Souci, the favorite residence
of Frederick the Great.   The latter edifice is far from
imposing, being a long, low building, erected on the summit
of a terrace, reached from the park by a flight of steps.

All who have climbed
this staircase from
the fountains will
recollect the
orange-trees on
either side. Fred-
erick, who took
great interest in
this garden, com-
plained once to the
minister from France
that in so cold a climate
his oranges and olives would

THE PALACE OF SANS SOUCI.

not thrive. The courtier hesitated for a moment, at a loss for a reply; for it was painfully evident that Frederick had told the exact truth. At last, however, he had recourse to diplomacy and answered: "Your Majesty may at least console yourself with the thought that, however it may be with your orange-trees, your laurels can never fade."

Above a window in the centre of this little villa is inscribed the name bestowed upon it by Frederick, — *Sans Souci,* "Free from Care"; for here the Prussian sovereign, warrior though he was, desired to lay aside his sword, and become a royal poet and philosopher, dividing his time between music, literature, and the society of intellectual friends and gay companions.

THE MUSIC-ROOM.

The villa of Sans Souci consists of merely a single row of apartments connected with one another, the central room being the dining-hall, the floor of which is of marble mosaic. Here, Frederick gave the dinner-parties which became so famous, not for the wines and viands that he furnished, but for the wit and intellectual discourse contributed by the King and his illustrious guests. In the Berlin National Gallery hangs a painting representing such a scene. Another apartment was used by Frederick for a music-room, and here were given the private concerts, at which Emanuel Bach would play upon the spinet, and other musicians on the violin and 'cello, while the King, with rare skill, played the flute.

On my last visit to Potsdam, the custodian of Sans Souci informed me that young Emperor William had given here, the night before, a private musical after the style of those which Frederick used to give, and that he himself had attempted to play the flute in imitation of his great ancestor, while the invited guests, as well as the Emperor, had been arrayed in the wigs and costumes of a century ago.

THE ORANGERY, POTSDAM.

Among the distinguished literary men whom Frederick gathered about him, after being freed from the mad tyranny of his father, was Voltaire; and the traveler can still behold at Sans Souci the suite of rooms assigned to him during his famous visit to Frederick, which ended so unhappily for them both. The fascination which the genius of Voltaire exerted over Frederick is easily explained. On account of his unfortunate bringing up under a boorish father, who detested everything that was French, Frederick had learned to hate, on the other hand, almost everything that was German; and, being naturally bright, scholarly, and vivacious, he greatly admired the famous writers of France who then dominated the literary world. Hence, it is not surprising that the young Prince entered

INTERIOR OF THE ORANGERY.

into correspondence with Voltaire, the most celebrated poet of his time. The latter was then fifty years of age, and, pleased with Frederick's admiration, knew how to increase it by skilful flattery. Thus, he wrote to the young Prince: "I believe that Berlin will one day take precedence over Athens; for Frederick is already greater than Socrates." With such a commencement their friendship rapidly increased.

When Voltaire accepted Frederick's invitation to visit him at Potsdam, the pretext that he gave for

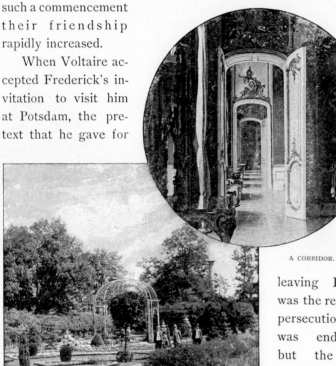

A CORRIDOR.

THE GARDENS OF SANS SOUCI.

leaving France was the religious persecution he was enduring; but the fact seems to be that he had a secret commission from the French Government to try to bring Frederick over to the side of France. At first, Voltaire seemed very happy at the Prussian Court, and wrote home the most flattering accounts of Frederick. It is possible, however, that some of his enthusiasm was due to the suspicion that his letters were

opened and read; for there is no doubt that, after a little
time, he found the atmosphere of Sans Souci thoroughly un-
congenial. Nor is this strange; for, though the intellectual
tastes of the King and his French guest were similar, their
dispositions were entirely different. They would have still
admired each other at a distance, but propinquity proved fatal
to their friendship. Ere many months had passed, the situa-

THE STAIRCASE AND TERRACES.

tion became critical, and they threw bitter and sarcastic words
like thunderbolts at each other. In this Voltaire had, on the
whole, the advantage; for never has the man existed who could
infuse so much poison into a sneer, as could Voltaire. Thus,
in reference to correcting the French verses which Frederick wanted him to criticise, he remarked, "The King
sends me his soiled linen to wash." He also sarcastically
said of the Prussians, that in their language they made up

for the scarcity of their ideas by the length of their words and the superfluity of their consonants. What wonder, then, that in return Frederick declared that Voltaire was a blackguard and a consummate rascal? "I am amazed," he wrote, "that so much talent does not make a better man. He deserves to be flogged for his actions. He has behaved in a most unworthy manner; he deserves to be branded on Parnassus, and it is a pity that such a worthless soul should be linked to so glorious a genius. Still," he added, "I will not express my feelings to him, for I require his aid in studying the French language; fine things may be learned even from a vaga-

STATUE OF FREDERICK THE GREAT.

ON THE TERRACE.

bond. I want to know how to write his French. What do
I care for his morals?"

Voltaire, on the other hand, wrote to his niece: "Co-
quettes, kings, and poets are accustomed to flattery. Frederick combines these three characters. It is not possible
that truth can pierce this triple wall of self-esteem."

FREDERICK IN HIS STUDY.

It is easy to see, therefore, that these men could not
live together. The ties which bound them would not
endure such constant irritation as their daily intercourse
occasioned, and soon snapped in anger. It was on the esplanade, in front of the great palace of Potsdam, while Frederick was reviewing his troops, that Voltaire and his patron
met for the last time. An officer approached the King and

said: "Sire, Monsieur Voltaire has come to take his leave
of you." Frederick turned toward his former friend and
remarked quietly: "Are you then resolved to go?" "Sire,"
replied Voltaire, "the state of my health requires my
departure." "In that case," said the King, "I wish you *bon
voyage.*" In this way separated (never to meet again) two
of the brightest minds in Europe, each having committed the
mistake so often made before and since their time, of thinking that a brilliant intellect, when brought into terms of
intimacy, must of necessity command love because it so
easily wins admiration.

The Royal Palace in the town of Potsdam was, also, frequently occupied by Frederick, particularly on State occasions,
for the villa of Sans Souci was little else than his private

THE OLD PALACE AT POTSDAM.

apartments. Here he received ambassadors from other lands, and one may still see here, adjoining his library, the secret cabinet where Frederick used to dine in private with his guests. The room is very small, and furnished in red satin with gold trimmings. In the middle of the room is a round table, the centre of which was arranged to detach itself from the outer circle of the table, and to descend through the floor into the kitchen below. The necessary food and dishes would be placed upon it, and it would rise again to its former place. The object of this ingenious mechanism was to avoid the presence of servants, thus enabling the King and his guests to converse without danger of being overheard.

THE TREE OF PETITIONS.

Not far from Sans Souci stands an aged oak, known as the Tree of Petitions; for on this Frederick desired to have his subjects fasten their petitions, which were removed only by himself. Among them, he once discovered a complaint that the Roman Catholic schools had been used to convert Protestant children to Catholicism. Frederick returned the following reply : " All religions must be tolerated, but none must make unjust encroachments upon the others. In this country every man must get to heaven his own way." The good sense of these words, so rare in those days, electrified his people, drew the attention of the whole world to Frederick, and gave him great renown.

THE ROYAL PALACE.

This generous toleration was shown by him in many ways. Thus, as he was returning one day to Potsdam on horseback, he saw a crowd examining a picture posted high up on a wall. The King requested his groom to see what it was. The man returned, and in a faltering voice explained that it was a shameful caricature, portraying the King hiding food away from his half-starved subjects. "Take it down," said Frederick, "and put it lower, so that the people may not strain their necks in looking at it." The crowd heard what he said, and, laughing heartily, tore the placard into shreds, and shouted to their sovereign, as he rode on toward the palace, "Long live our Fritz! Our Fritz forever!" Another interesting relic of those days at Sans Souci is the windmill about which Frederick had his famous controversy. He wished, as is well

THE ART GALLERY.

known, to purchase and tear it down, since the unsightly object annoyed him; but its owner refused to sell, and was even successful in a lawsuit with his Majesty. Whereupon Frederick generously turned about and gave him money wherewith to enlarge and improve his mill. It still remains in the possession of the descendants of the miller. Some years ago, its owner, being pecuniarily embarrassed, desired to sell it; but old Kaiser William, learning of it, instantly sent him money to relieve him, saying: "Never dispose of

THE OLD MILL.

that property. In your family it is a part of Prussian history."

If Sans Souci was "free from care," it was also free from luxury. During his reign of more than forty years, except when absent in his numerous wars, Frederick's habits scarcely varied. In winter, as well as in summer, his servants were commanded to awaken him every morning at four o'clock, and if he did not instantly arise, to put wet towels on his head. He slept upon a plain, camp bedstead made of iron. A slouch hat served him for a nightcap. Only his library was richly furnished. When he had finished with his secretaries after breakfast, he walked an hour or two, pencil and book in hand, with a number of dogs playing around him. In the evening, his delight was a private concert. Frederick had brilliant powers of conversation, and these were never better shown than in the famous suppers which he gave at Sans Souci, lasting from half-past eight to midnight. As a rule, only distinguished gentlemen were invited to these repasts; for Frederick's favorites were always men of intellectual ability. He never cared especially for the society of women, and, with the exception of his sister, few were admitted to his Court.

There is a pathos in the closing part of Frederick's life at Sans Souci. After a reign of forty-six years, he found himself, at the age of seventy-four, childless and almost friend-less, on the verge of the grave. It was on the terrace in front of this villa that, shortly before his death, the old warrior was brought out in his arm-chair, surrounded by his dogs, to bask in the sun. Looking up at the great luminary, the dying monarch murmured, " Perhaps I shall soon be nearer to thee than now."

THE CATHEDRAL.

Close by the palace of Sans Souci, at the end of the terrace,

are the graves of Frederick's favorite dogs.   Every one knows
how fond he was of these pets.   He would allow them to tear
his curtains and furniture into shreds, merely laughing at the
havoc, and saying: "It is a less expensive weakness than
most monarchs have.   A Marquise de Pompadour would cost
me a great deal more, and would not be so fond or faithful.
My dogs," he added, "are the only true, faithful friends I
have ever known."   He thought of them even at the last
moment of his life; for, as he sat in the arm-chair in which
he died, literally gasp-   ing for breath, he

THE SPREE.

noticed one of his dogs
near him shivering
with cold, and ordered a blanket to be thrown over it.   A few
minutes later, after a severe attack of coughing, he whispered,
"The mountain is passed.   We shall be better now."   These
were his last words.   It was midnight.   Two hours later the
stars looked down as usual on Sans Souci, but the spirit of
its royal master had departed.

     Filled with these memories of Frederick, no one will leave
Potsdam without paying a visit to a plain edifice, known as
the Garrison Church, because the soldiers stationed in the town
are required to attend service here.   Within this building

A CONCERT AT SANS SOUCI.

Frederick the Great is buried, and
on the walls, in honor of the
man whose ashes rest beneath
its roof, are hung the battle-
flags taken by Frederick
from Austria and Russia,
as well as some secured
by his descendants from
Austria in 1865, and from
France in 1871. Other
strange decorations for a
structure dedicated to the
Prince of Peace are swords and
lances, placed among the flags;
and at each of the four corners of
the organ are drums and trumpets,
the former having figures wound by springs to beat them
when the instrument is played.

FREDERICK THE GREAT.

At midnight, on the 4th of November, 1805, Alexander,
Tsar of Russia, Frederick William III., and Queen Louisa
stood within this church, and, clasping hands above the
hero's tomb, solemnly pledged themselves to a coalition
against Napoleon. How inscrutable is the future! Just one
year later, on the same day of the month, and almost at
the same hour, Napoleon in his turn visited this tomb of
Frederick, having meantime overwhelmingly defeated the
armies of Prussia, Austria, and Russia. The flight of the
Prussians from Potsdam had been so hasty that many relics
of the great Frederick were left behind. Among them was
the sword which he had worn during the Seven Years' War.
It lay alone upon the warrior's casket. Napoleon had a
great admiration for Frederick's military genius, and, as he
took his sword into his hands, he exclaimed to the officers
of his suite: "Gentlemen, this was one of the greatest com-

manders of whom history has made mention. If he were
alive to-day, I should not be standing here." Dust had
settled on the royal sarcophagus, and in this the French
Emperor thoughtfully traced the letter "N." Then he
ordered that the sword of the Prussian King be sent to Paris
to decorate the Hôtel des Invalides. General Rapp, who

NAPOLEON AT THE TOMB OF FREDERICK.

stood beside him, ventured to express surprise that Napoleon
did not keep the relic for his own use; whereupon Bonaparte
turned to him with a smile and, playfully pulling his ear,
remarked, "Have I not, then, a sword of my own?" Napoleon, furthermore, manifested his respect for Frederick by
ordering that, in honor of his memory, Potsdam should be
exempted from paying any military contribution to the conqueror.

Another prominent edifice at Potsdam is called the "New

Palace," because it was built by Frederick the Great, in addition to the royal residences he already possessed, to prove that his resources were not exhausted by his Seven Years' War with Russia, Austria, and France.

In this New Palace, however, the tourist comes upon more recent souvenirs than those of Sans Souci, since in this structure he may pass from recollections of Frederick the Great to those of Frederick the Noble, — "Our Fritz," as he was fondly called, but who is now

THE MARBLE GALLERY, POTSDAM.

enrolled in history as Frederick III. Here on the 15th of June, 1888, in the room whose windows are the fourth and fifth to the left of the doorway on the ground floor, the father of the present Emperor breathed his last.

This illustrious Prince seemed the very ideal of a high-minded and noble-hearted sovereign. At the conclusion of the war with France, in 1871, it would have been hard to find a more perfect specimen of manly vigor. He was called, indeed, by some "the handsomest man in Europe."

Tall, muscular, and finely formed, he had the fair complexion, golden beard, and clear blue eyes of the old Teutons. Every one knows how gallantly he bore himself in both the Austrian and French campaigns, receiving on the field of battle, from his father's hands, the highest of all German decorations. Yet, notwithstanding his ability and courage,

THE CROWN PRINCE'S PALACE.

he was heartily opposed to bloodshed, and even at the time of the triumphal entry into Paris, he remarked to his officers: "Gentlemen, I do not like war. If I ever reign, I will never make it." Perhaps this love of peace, and the concessions he was willing to make for it, formed the starting-point of that antagonism which existed so long between himself and Bismarck.

"OUR FRITZ."

The life of Frederick III., as Crown Prince, was an exceedingly difficult one, for he was not in sympathy with many of his father's and Prince Bismarck's views. He made, however, no active opposition, but waited patiently for years, until as Emperor he could bring about those constitutional reforms which, in his judgment, were so greatly needed. But, "Man proposes, God disposes." When the old Emperor, at the age of ninety-one years, approached the valley of the shadow of death, and murmured as his last words, "Fritz, dear Fritz," his son and successor was not in Berlin, but far away beyond the Alps in the Italian village of San Remo, death-stricken himself, and already feeling, day and night, that fatal clutch upon his throat which no professional skill was able to relax. The wife of Frederick, who, previous to her marriage, had been, as the eldest

THE CROWN PRINCE AT SAN REMO.

daughter of Victoria, Princess Royal of England, is in all respects a noble woman, unostentatious, amiable, refined, and with decided intellectual ability. Both she and her husband were liberal patrons of art, literature, and music. For several years the philosopher Strauss was one of her regular correspondents, and at his death her portrait hung above his bed. Among her accomplishments is that of sculpture, and a marble bust of great fidelity and beauty (the product of her chisel) was given a permanent place in the Berlin Museum. It is not surprising, therefore, that such a woman was able to win and retain the love and admiration of her husband, and that he consulted with her freely on both public and private matters, and showed her an attention and devotion rarely exhibited in Germany toward the fair sex.

It is a pleasure to remember that the heroic, patient, liberalminded Frederick III. lived long enough to reach Berlin and hold the sceptre in his hands for at least

THE EMPRESS FREDERICK.

ninety days. Ill as he was these days were not misspent. Although he knew well that his son shared Bismarck's sentiments, and though he saw with inexpressible regret that any liberal policy, which he might start, would be undone the moment he should die, still, with a natural desire to leave at least a little influence for good upon his realm, he made several changes and expressed views, which clearly indicated what he would have done, had his life been prolonged. For instance, to show his disapproval of the Jewish persecution

LEIPZIG STREET.

EMPEROR WILLIAM II.

then prevalent in Prussia, the first man chosen by him to receive the famous order of the Black Eagle, was a Hebrew.

Frederick's noble face presented a pathetic picture, when his long struggle with disease had ended. The traces of his sufferings were still visible, and made even those who most loved him glad that he was finally at rest. Aside from the pain which he heroically endured, what must have been his disappointment in giving up one of the most brilliant thrones on earth, and in resigning the sceptre to his son, after so many years of waiting, and just at the moment when he was on the point of carrying out his life-long hopes and aspirations! Yet through it all he showed the same sweet, patient, uncomplaining spirit to the end. What could be more pathetic than the words traced on his tablet for his son to read, " Learn to suffer without complaining." What wonder that his surgeon, Doctor Mackenzie, could say of him, "Thus passed

A ROOM IN THE CROWN PRINCE'S PALACE.

away the noblest specimen of humanity, whom it was ever my privilege to see."

There have been few scenes in the history of Prussian royalty more touching than that which occurred in the Palace of Charlottenburg, when this illustrious sovereign, prevented by ill health from following his father's body to the grave, stood at the window and watched the funeral procession of old Kaiser William wind through the park to the imperial mausoleum. He must have known then that the hour of his own departure could not be far distant; and solemn, indeed, must have been his thoughts, as he stood speechless and alone, in royal isolation, gazing upon a funeral pageant in which all other members of the royal household, including even his own wife and children, were participating, but from which he, the reigning sovereign and son of the dead Emperor, was excluded.

VON MOLTKE.

In a beautiful structure near Sans Souci, known as Friedenskirche or the Church of Peace, Frederick the Noble sleeps in death, beside two sons who died in childhood. It is an inspiring place for those who reverence manly qualities and upright character.

That Frederick III. loved peace rather than war is no proof that he was lacking in noble, chivalrous, and manly qualities; for the most famous warrior of recent times, Field-Marshal Von Moltke, wept beside his coffin, and mourned him as a pupil, man, and sovereign.

Closely adjoining the Thiergarten stands the house occu-

JÄGERSTRASSE AND THE BANK.

pied by Prince Bismarck, when he was a resident of Berlin.
Now that he lives in retirement on his estate near Hamburg, this building has merely an historic value to the
tourist; but there was a time, before the present Kaiser had
dispensed with Bismarck's services, when this plain, unpretentious dwelling almost rivaled in interest and importance the
abode of royalty.

It was here, for instance that, in 1878, the Berlin Con-
gress of European diplomats assembled for the settlement
of the Eastern question. A crowd of people often waited

THE RESIDENCE OF PRINCE BISMARCK.

near this residence, in the hope of seeing its owner; for,
notwithstanding his occasional arrogance, no one could
doubt, in Bismarck's later life, his popularity with the German people. When, for example, he appeared in public at
the reception given in Berlin to the King of Italy, the
streets were crowded with humanity, and the cry of
"Bismarck! Bismarck!" was louder than that which greeted
either King or Emperor. On that occasion, when Bismarck's

carriage turned into Linden, the roar of acclamations became
deafening.

In 1885, also, the Germans made of Bismarck's seven-
tieth birthday almost a national festival.   Four thousand

THE SCENE AT VERSAILLES.

veteran soldiers and ten thousand students from all parts
of the Fatherland joined in a procession to his house, and,
in the evening, the greatest number of torch-bearers ever
united in Germany took part in the celebration.

On these occasions, as on subsequent anniversaries of his
birth, it was not merely Bismarck as an individual whom
his compatriots thus saluted.   He is to the Germans a conspicuous reminder of their nation's glory.   The sight of him
recalls to them a hundred scenes forever memorable in their
history.   They see him as he appeared when, on the morn-

ing following the battle of Sedan, he sat beside the Emperor
of France. A mouse within the clutches of a cat could not
have better typified then the situation of Napoleon III.; for
in his very declaration of war he had been merely a puppet
in Prince Bismarck's hand, acting as Bismarck pulled the
string, until he found himself a helpless prisoner, his individual destiny and that of France depending largely upon
Bismarck's will. Nor is this all. When the good Prussians
greet their Chancellor with cheers, they see him also in his
greater hour of triumph at Versailles, when he declared his
ultimatum to the dismayed and hopeless diplomats, Jules

" AFTER SEDAN."

Favre and Thiers, demanding unrelentingly the provinces of
Alsace and Lorraine, and an indemnity of five thousand
million francs. Enormous as this was, Prince Bismarck was
in one respect outwitted by the Frenchmen. In drawing up

that most humiliating treaty, Thiers con-
trived to insert an apparently innocent
clause, whereby the time of paying the
indemnity was left to France. This
was deemed by Germany unimportant,
for Bismarck never dreamed that such
a sum could be collected before the
expiration of ten years; but in less
than one year, Thiers had paid the
last centime, and every Prussian soldier had
left the soil of France.

BISMARCK.

There can be no doubt that Bismarck's influence will
be felt in Europe for centuries. Moreover, time will gradually soften his defects, and show posterity a man who, notwithstanding many faults, was perfectly devoted to the
Fatherland.

He knew exactly what he wanted, and was resolved to
do three things which he at last accomplished: to crush
the independence of Germany's minor sovereigns; to render
Austria subordinate to Prussia; and,
finally, to make of Germany one
mighty empire with the King
of Prussia as its ruler. In
doing this he did not hesitate
as to the means employed.
He was a believer not in
long discussions, but in ac-
tion. Oratory he considered
a waste of time. "The
great questions of the day,"
he said in 1862, "are settled
not by speeches and the de-
cisions of majorities, but by blood
and iron."

BISMARCK AND THE YOUNG KAISER.

In memory of all that he has done, it is not strange that
Germany admires Bismarck, the last survivor of the giants
of that stirring epoch. It is true, like most great men, he
shows to better advantage on a pedestal, than under close

VON MOLTKE AND BISMARCK.

inspection. He was cruel and relentless; so was Richelieu.
He was cunning and revengeful; so was Mazarin. He
cherished great ambitions and provoked great wars; so did
Napoleon. But first, last, and always he has been com-
pletely and unselfishly loyal; first to Prussia, secondly to

Germany.   Hence, since perfection is not found in poor
humanity, the portrait-gallery of the world's great men,
whom Time and History select and classify, will evermore
contain the face of that great master of diplomacy and
founder of the German Empire, Otto Von Bismarck.

SCHILLER AND GOETHE.

VIENNA

VIENNA

THE EMPEROR OF AUSTRIA.

VIENNA is one of the oldest cities of Europe. When St. Petersburg was a swamp, and Berlin a straggling village on a sandy plain, Vienna had been for centuries a powerful metropolis, standing as Moscow stands to-day,— a kind of frontier city, an eastern outpost of European civilization. Only two hundred years ago it was the principal bulwark of defense that checked the armies of the Moslems which had victoriously swept along

the Danube, captured Belgrade and Budapest, and made of
Hungary a Turkish province.

Vienna, therefore, at one extremity of Europe, and Tours
at the other, mark the two points of the great Moslem
crescent of invasion into Christian territory; and, as in
France, upon the borders of the Loire, in 732, Charles
Martel "hammered" the army of the Saracens and drove
it southward into Spain, so on the banks of the Danube, in
1683, John Sobieski and his Pol-

A GENERAL VIEW OF VIENNA.

ish army aided the Viennese to roll back the advancing wave
of Turkish conquest.

The history of Vienna reaches back, however, to times
far more remote than these. The Romans, early in the
Christian era, had established on this spot a settlement
known as Vindobona, and here it was, in the year 180, that
Marcus Aurelius, the noblest of Rome's Emperors, breathed
his last, having given from his death-bed as the password
for the night the sublime expression, "*Æquanimitas.*"

PANORAMA OF VIENNA.

Vienna not only has the charm of an important history, it is also one of the most beautiful of European capitals, and has been called the Paris of Austria. There are, indeed, many points of similarity between the capitals of Austria and France. Both were once Roman settlements. In each a Cæsar has resided: the Emperor Julian living in one; Marcus Aurelius dying in the other. Both are preëminently beautiful and brilliant, and both are located on promi- nent rivers which, never- theless, flow in opposite directions. The Seine glides westward to the broad Atlantic, its cur- rent turned toward the New World. The Dan- ube, on the contrary, rolls eastward, to lose itself in that historic sea, which Xenophon's retreating thousands greeted with delight.

THE FRANZ JOSEPH FOUNTAIN.

This difference is significant; for not unlike their rivers are the capitals themselves. Paris in all its tendencies is Occidental, radical, and modern. Vienna — residence of an Emperor, who rules not only Austria, but Hungary as well, and has his hand outstretched to grasp the prov- inces between his kingdom and the Bosphorus — looks down the Danube toward the Orient, and has a trace of the con- servatism and the languor of the East. Moreover, both

these capitals have more than once been closely bound
together in their history.   Again and again have French
and Austrian soldiers met in desperate conflict in Austria,

ON THE OLD BASTIONS

Bavaria, Italy,
France, and Swit-
zerland. Yet from
Vienna went
forth, to be Queen
of France, the
beautiful and ill-
fated Marie An-
toinette; and it
was to Napoleon
that the Austrian
Emperor, Francis,
gave in marriage
his daughter,
Marie Louise.

Vienna has greatly improved in appearance during the
reign of the present Emperor, Franz Joseph.   Less than
half a century ago, high walls and a deep moat surrounded
this old Austrian capital; but its increasing life and energy
finally burst these barriers, and poured forth in a mighty
flood on the adjoining plain.   Its ramparts then were seen to
be as useless and superfluous as an outgrown suit of armor.
Accordingly, the moat was filled, and the broad battlements
were either leveled to the ground or transformed into terraces
and promenades, whence one obtains extensive and delightful
views.

The first impression, therefore, that the traveler receives,
as he drives through Vienna, is that of two concentric circles, the inner one reminding him of the Vienna of the
past, the outer delighting him as the Vienna of the present; and the connecting link between them is a circular

promenade constructed on the ancient fortifications, and now known as the Ringstrasse.

It would perhaps be injudicious to make a minute comparison between this and the Parisian boulevards. The latter are more animated, and, in the neighborhood of the Avenue de l'Opéra, are unrivaled; but certain portions of the Viennese thoroughfare undoubtedly surpass some sec-

THE HOTEL METROPOLE.

tions of the boulevards of Paris, and, as a rule, the buildings on the Ringstrasse are far superior to those between the Church of the Madeleine and the Place de la Bastille. Moreover, the circular form of the Austrian promenade imparts to it a charm that no straight avenue can possibly possess. Imagine, then, the Ringstrasse to be a splendid

ON THE RINGSTRASSE.

girdle, dividing, yet uniting, old and new Vienna, lined with
imposing modern structures, bordered by handsome parks
and souares, and containing a bridle-path, two driveways,
spacious sidewalks, and well-shaded promenades. One
should, at first, drive around the entire circuit to gain a
general impression of its beauty and extent, and then retrace
the curving route by sections, observing carefully the architectural gems with which it is adorned.

These buildings, having been constructed recently, present a fresh and elegant appearance, and are remarkable for
their fine proportions and their immense amount of sculptured ornamentation. One after another, they excite our

admiration, and when we have surveyed them all, we find
it difficult to award to any one of them the honor of

supremacy. The
House of Parlia-
ment, for exam-
ple, is a triumph
of modern archi-
tecture, being a
reproduction of
old   Grecian
styles adapted to
modern require-
ments, and a
magnificent edi-

A CORNER OF THE HOUSE OF PARLIAMENT.

fice of white marble, its walls enriched by columns, statues,
and reliefs, and with colossal groups in bronze upon the roof.

Not far away stands the imposing University, with nine
courts, elegant reception halls, marble staircases, an extensive
library, great lecture-rooms their walls embellished with
wood-carving and historic paintings, and a reading-room with

APPROACH TO THE PARLIAMENT HOUSE.

seats for three hundred persons. This noble institution has about six thousand students, and a faculty of about four hundred professors, some of whom enjoy a world-wide reputation.

Rivaling the University in interest is the Court Theatre, one of the most imposing structures on the Ringstrasse, and one of the finest temples of dramatic art that man has yet produced. Too much detailed description of these edifices would be monotonous, yet it should

A CORNER OF THE RINGSTRASSE.

be remembered that this admirably proportioned building is of white marble, and abounds in statues and reliefs, which tell in sculptured lines the progress of the drama from the earliest times. The grand relief on the façade, portraying the "Triumph of Bacchus," is one of the finest productions of the century. Everything is admirably managed in this theatre for the comfort of its patrons. Before and after the performance, polite, uniformed officials stand on the steps to assist those who arrive in carriages to alight; and, once past the marble

THE UNIVERSITY.

corridor, one finds a number of ticket offices to obviate
crowding.   The cloak-rooms, too, are large, with numerous
attendants to prevent delay; while courteous ushers are at
hand to lead the way into the richly decorated auditorium.
This theatre is, of course, subsidized by the Government;

THE ROYAL THEATRE.

and dramas of the highest order are given here in a style
worthy of the magnificent edifice in which they are produced.
    Another remarkable feature of the circular boulevard is
the Votive Church, whose delicately sculptured and open-
work towers — three hundred and twenty-five feet in height
— remind one of the cathedral of Burgos in Spain.   Designed in florid Gothic style, and exquisitely proportioned,
it is the most beautiful ecclesiastical structure in Vienna,
and is deservedly dear to the Viennese as commemorating
the escape of the present Emperor, Franz Joseph, from

assassination in 1853. For, popular and beloved though the
Austrian Kaiser is, there was then found a wretch who
wished to murder him, and would probably have succeeded
in his attempt, had not the gold lace on the collar of the
Emperor's military coat turned the point of the knife, as
the assassin thrust it at his throat.

On leaving this church, I exclaimed to my companions,
"Surely there can be nothing else upon this promenade
approaching in magnificence of architecture what we
have already seen." Yet, at
a little distance, another modern building greeted us, which
we confessed was entitled to
an equal rank with any of
its rivals. This was the City
Hall, the cost of which was
more than seven million dollars. Even at the risk of
being tedious, I must enumerate a few of the remarkable
features of this edifice. Its
massive tower, adorned with
fine reliefs, reaches
the height of three
hundred and twenty
feet, and holds aloft
the gilded statue of
a standard-bearer.
Within its en-
closure are no
less   than
seven court-
yards, some
of them sur-

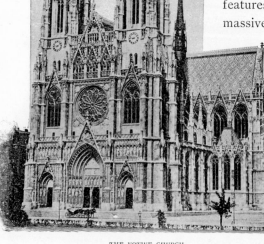

THE VOTIVE CHURCH.

THE CITY HALL.

rounded by arcades, resembling cloisters. Two stairways of white marble, lined
with gilded balustrades, lead
to a series of municipal
apartments which I believe
to be unequaled in any similar structure in the world.
One of these, the Historical
Museum of Vienna, will
repay careful scrutiny. Here
are gathered almost all
imaginable relics of the city
from the days of the Romans
to the present time, including
ancient tombs and statues,
souvenirs of Maria Theresa,
former costumes of the
nobility, old instruments of
torture, portraits of famous
poets and musicians, the
pianos of Mozart and Schu-

A PORTAL OF THE VOTIVE CHURCH.

bert, and the death-masks of Beethoven and Haydn; together
with nearly fifteen hundred
specimens of ancient
weapons and armor, and
relics of the wars
between the Austrians
and Turks.

There is, in Vienna,
as there should be in
all large cities, a censor-
ship of architecture. People

THE CITY HALL FRONT.

THE RECEPTION-ROOM IN THE CITY HALL.

are not allowed to build precisely as they like, without the least regard to the property of their neighbors or the æsthetic

THE STAIRCASE IN THE PALACE OF JUSTICE.

appearance of the city. The good of the community is not sacrificed to an excess of individual liberty. Moreover, here, as in Paris, attention is invariably paid to perspective, and every public building, statue, or fountain is placed so that it can be seen to advantage. With the exception of Washington, this rule has been too seldom observed in American cities; but in Vienna the eye is always pleased with long

perspectives of taste-
fully decorated build-
ings, which usually form
an avenue of approach
to some grand object
at the terminus. In
fact, to such an extent
is the idea of municipal
embellishment carried,
that prizes have been
offered to those who
should erect the hand-

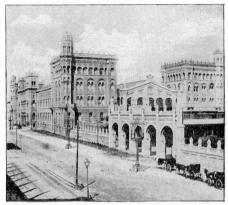

A VIENNESE RAILWAY STATION.

somest edifices on certain streets or squares. By one who
did not understand this sentiment of civic pride, the principal
railway station of Vienna might be, at first, mistaken for a
Government building, so palatial are its dimensions and so
imposingly designed are its huge, crenelated walls and
towers. It follows, as a matter of course, that the "sky-
scrapers" which mar the beauty of many of our cities, not so

THE PALACE OF JUSTICE.

much from their materials or design, as from the hideous
irregularity in the sky-line which they cause, are never seen
in Vienna, since the Government regulates there the height of
the buildings in proportion to the breadth of the streets. We
are accustomed to regard New York as a handsome city,
architecturally, and so it is in spots; but even on Fifth
Avenue, within a block of some of the best residences, one
sees occasionally miserable wooden structures side by side
with beautiful stone houses. This in Vienna would be impossible.

VIENNESE SHOPS.

One practical result of making streets beautiful and artistic
is that they become places of enjoyment for the citizen. It
is not altogether a difference of temperament that causes
Europeans to spend so much time seated on spacious sidewalks, under the awnings of cafés. If our streets were made
as attractive as theirs, we would, also, spend more time in them.

THE INTERIOR OF THE OPERA HOUSE.

To the Parisians and the Viennese their sidewalks are, like the *foyers* of their theatres, places in which to meet their friends, chat with them for an hour, and view, meantime, the passing life and gaiety of the town. We, on the contrary, stay almost altogether in our offices or houses, and often regard our streets as disagreeable thoroughfares to hurry through as fast as possible, going from one place to the other.

Impressed with the array of stately edifices in Vienna, the tourist naturally asks at first, " Where are the private houses of its citizens?"

THE GRAND HOTEL.

But, with very rare exceptions, there are no private houses in Vienna. One sees no blocks of single residences, as in New York or Philadelphia; nor pretty separate dwellings, each with its private lot of land, such as we find in most of our large western cities. The grand residential structures, in Vienna, are neither more nor less than apartment houses; and, instead of being the exception as in America, they here form the rule. Many of them are furnished much

more elegantly than our own, and are adorned with paintings, statuary, and frescos; but in such points of comfort as
steam-heat, electric lights, attractive bath-rooms, abundant hot
and cold water, and other features of our best apartments,
those of Vienna are inferior.

Another superb edifice on the Ringstrasse is the Grand
Opera House, which yields in splendor only to its Paris rival.

THE OPERA HOUSE.

In fact, if one has never seen the latter, the Austrian temple
of music will seem unsurpassed in the sumptuous decorations
of its staircase, portico and *foyer;* while the auditorium, which
has a seating capacity for two thousand five hundred, is decorated far more pleasantly and with less ostentatious gilding
than that of Paris.

Late comers to a performance in this opera house are not
allowed to disturb the audience already assembled. No one is
permitted to take his seat during the overture; and in Wagner's

THE LOGGIA OF THE OPERA HOUSE.

operas, where there is no intermission between the overture and the first act, those who come late are not allowed to go to their seats until the curtain falls. In the case of the "Götterdämmerung," where the first act lasts nearly an hour and a half, this rule must cause considerable inconvenience ; but, after all, it is well to insist on punctuality, and such heroic measures are, no doubt, necessary to enforce it. There is no good reason why several thousand specta-

THE ENTRANCE.

tors should have their attention diverted from an opera, which they have paid a high price to hear, by the arrival of persons who are careless or thoughtless enough to come late. Sometimes, of course, a ticket-holder may be unavoidably detained ; but in

that case it is better that he should suffer than all the rest of
the audience. It is needless to add that, at the Vienna opera,
no woman is allowed to annoy people by wearing a large hat.

The structures which have been already mentioned would
of themselves be sufficient to make the Ringstrasse architecturally famous, but these by no means constitute all the wonderful buildings on this prom-   enade. Thus, opposite the
entrance to the Palace   Garden, are two imperial
museums — gigantic   structures, which cor-
respond to each other   perfectly in size and

AUSTRIAN SOLDIERS PASSING THE MUSEUM.

ornamentation. One is devoted to Natural History, while the
other contains the immensely valuable art collections of the
imperial family, which were formerly distributed in various
localities, but are now gathered under one roof.

THE MARIA THERESA MONUMENT.

Between these great museums intervenes a square, adorned
with flower-beds, colossal statues, and marble fountains, and in
the centre of this attractive area stands the majestic monument erected, in 1888, to the memory of Maria Theresa, by
the Emperor Franz Joseph.   The traveler hardly knows which

SIDE VIEW OF MARIA THERESA'S STATUE.

to admire most,
the statue of the
Empress, or the
elaborate pedes-
tal.   The latter
is of marble, but
the seated-figure
of Maria Theresa,
nineteen feet in
height,   is   of
bronze, and rep-
resents the sover-
eign holding the
sceptre   in   one
hand, while she
extends the other
in gracious salu-
tation.

This   noble
work of art is to
Vienna what the equestrian statue of Frederick the Great
is to Berlin, — a sculptured epitome of Austrian history
during the reign of the illustrious Empress; for around
the pedestal, which is forty-three feet in height, are equestrian figures, life-sized statues and reliefs of the most prominent generals, statesmen, jurists, physicians, historians and
musicians who adorned that age, and, in their different
ways, contributed to the glory of the sovereign whose statue
is enthroned in majesty above them.   Among these I no-

THE FRANZ JOSEPH QUAY.

ticed, particularly, the figures of the composers Gluck and
Haydn holding young Mozart by the hand, and the conspic-
uous statue of Maria Theresa's famous premier, Prince
Kaunitz, whose characteristics have been well portrayed in
Louisa Mülbach's historical novel, "Joseph II. and his Court."

In regard to Kaunitz, however, truth is stranger than fiction.
In personal appearance he was tall and commanding, with
well-cut features, clear blue eyes, and a complexion of which
he took as much care as a society belle. He always wore
an enormous wig, which, in his later years, was fastened just
above his eyebrows, to conceal the wrinkles on his forehead.
To the powdering of this important article of dress he paid
great attention. Every morning he used to walk between two
rows of servants, each armed with a vase full of different
colored powder. This they would pour in succession over

his wig as he passed, so that it finally exhibited a harmony of varied tints which never failed to astonish all beholders. Kaunitz was so sure of his political position that he affected to despise court etiquette. Thus, he refused to wear the Austrian court costume, and always appeared in a Paris-made suit, consisting of a black silk coat and knee-breeches, black silk stockings, and shoes with diamond buckles. In fact, he was such a worshiper of everything French, that all his clothes, linen, jewelry, and furniture were sent to him from Paris, and he invariably spoke in French except to those whom he knew to be absolutely unacquainted with that language.

Several stories of his arrogance are quite amusing. Thus, on one occasion, Kaunitz requested Gluck to rehearse one of his operas before him alone. Gluck muttered something about an audience being necessary, but the Prince promptly interrupted him. "M. Gluck," he said, "remember that quality is worth as much as quantity. I alone constitute an

VIENNESE ARCHITECTURE.

VIENNESE BARRACKS.

audience." His talents as a diplomat and chancellor were, nevertheless, so great that he was called the "Richelieu of Austria," and "The Driver of the European Coach," and kept his place at the head of the Austrian cabinet for forty years, — hence all his eccentricities and vanity were overlooked, and the Empress regarded him as her ablest counselor.

Standing before the monument of Maria Theresa, and studying her statue in connection with those of her illustrious subjects, it is a pleasure to recall some incidents of her career. Naturally, the first to present itself to one's memory is the thrilling episode in her life, which gives to the whole history of that age a touch of pathos and romantic beauty. Frederick the Great was then invading Silesia, and the ruler of Bavaria — who had also declared war against Austria — had already taken possession of the cities of

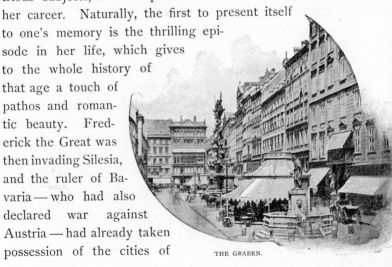

THE GRABEN.

Passau and Lintz, and was marching on Vienna. At this desperate crisis Maria Theresa appealed to her Hungarian subjects, and summoned their leaders to meet her at Presburg.

Clad in Hungarian costume, and wearing the iron crown of St. Stephen on her beautiful head, she entered the hall with slow, majestic tread, and stood before the throne. There, holding by the hand her little son (subsequently Joseph II.) she addressed the assembly in Latin, a language then in use among the Hungarians, and which Maria Theresa spoke with fluency. In a voice revealing at the same time her great distress, yet firm determination to

THE ENTRANCE TO THE MUSEUM OF THE ARSENAL.

resist injustice, she appealed to them: "Deserted by my friends, persecuted by my enemies, attacked by my relatives, my last resource is in your loyalty, your courage, and my own unyielding constancy. The time has come when the faithful hearts of Hungary must be tested before the eyes of the world. A crisis is at hand. The sword must be drawn, either in defense of your sovereign, or in support of her insulting enemies; but in the hearts of brave men, I have a refuge in the worst emergencies. I have chosen, therefore, this hour to place in your hands the persons of your sovereign and her son, who, in their extremity, look to you for protection."

MARIA THERESA.

These words, together with her beauty, majesty, and sorrow, roused the Hungarian nobles to the wildest enthusiasm, and drawing their sabres half-way from their scabbards, they flung them back to the hilt with a mighty shout that echoed through the building, as they cried, " Let us die for our *King*, Maria Theresa ! "

In personal appearance Maria Theresa was well-fitted for her exalted position. Her figure was stately, and in youth exquisitely proportioned; her arms and hands especially being of remarkable beauty; her face, a perfect oval, was lighted by large gray eyes that sparkled with vivacity; her hair was long and golden in color; her mouth was beautifully shaped, and a slightly aquiline nose heightened the commanding effect which her manner inspired. Moreover, her smile was charming, and her voice peculiarly sweet and clear. She did not plead her sex as an excuse for not performing all her duties as a sovereign; but, on the contrary, she conducted the affairs of State with energy, and spent many hours daily holding conferences and giving instructions to her ministers. In purely family affairs she was as thoroughly domestic as any *hausfrau* in a provincial town; and, though an affectionate, was a very exacting mother to her children, of whom she had sixteen, — five sons and eleven daughters. At Vienna she used to see them all three or four times

THE FRANZENSRING.

a day. She was likewise a most devoted wife, and from
the day of her husband's death she not only wore (for
sixteen years) the deepest mourning, but also had the
walls of her private apartments hung with black. Even
the season of the year in which he died was always sacred
to his memory; and during the whole month of August,
annually, she secluded herself from society and spent most
of the time in fasting and prayer. A short time before
she expired, as she was lying with her eyes closed in
silent prayer, an attendant whispered, " The Empress sleeps."

Maria Theresa in-
stantly opened
her eyes. " No,"
she said, " I do
not sleep. I have
been expecting
Death for sixteen
years, and when
he comes I wish
to meet him
awake."

No less than
four attractive
parks border the
Ringstrasse and
relieve it from
the possible mo-

THE STATUE OF FRANCIS I.

notony of an uninterrupted expanse of architecture. It is
delightful, on a pleasant afternoon or evening, to stroll
along this curving boulevard, and see so many thousands
peacefully enjoying out-door life in these resorts, — listening
to music, partaking of light refreshments, or sitting with
friends at little tables, before which moves an ever-changing
spectacle of pleasure.

THE CITY PARK.

In one of these gardens Strauss' famous
orchestra plays every night in summer, while
a military band alternates with it, so that the
music is uninterrupted during the entire evening. At
such a time, the traveler realizes that this is emphatically a city of simple, rational amusements. The Viennese are said to be the most musical people in the world.
At all events, Vienna has one hundred music schools and
sixty musical societies, and has been the home of Gluck,
Mozart, Beethoven, Wagner, Haydn, Millöcker, Schubert,
Brahms, Suppé, and the Strausses. The latter seem especially associated with Vienna, and rarely has there been seen
a more conspicuous instance of the heredity of genius
than in this family of musicians. Not only was the father,
Johann Strauss, a famous composer of waltzes and the con-

ductor of an orchestra, with which
he made a series of European
tours, but his three sons —
Johann (the "Waltz King"),
Eduard, and Joseph — have
followed in his footsteps;
and, together, these four men
have composed more than a
thousand pieces of dance-music,
of which Johann the younger has
contributed about four hundred
waltzes, besides numerous operettas.

JOHANN STRAUSS.

The Strausses were born in Vienna, and the Austrian capital,

STATUE OF SCHUBERT.

therefore, proudly
claims them as
her own. Their
works, although
popular the world
over, are specially
enjoyed in Vi-
enna; and if the
waltz is, as it is
sometimes called,
the poetry of mo-
tion, all the Vi-
ennese are gifted
poets in this re-
spect. A student
once assured me
that he had yet
to find in Vienna
a single person,
man or woman, in
any grade of so-

ciety, who was not something of a musician and a fine
dancer.

Every city, like every man, has its peculiarities sharply
defined and characteristic, which give it an individuality that is
well adapted to produce upon the traveler, who studies it in
its varying moods, a certain definite impression, unlike that
received by him from any other locality.

To the citizens of the Austrian capital, more than any
other people I have ever met, can be applied the almost
untranslatable adjective *gemüthlich*. The upper classes extend greetings with a quick, warm-hearted hospitality that is
in striking contrast to the cold reserve of northern Germany;
and in the middle and lower classes there seems to be a
characteristic, universal merriment delightful to behold. Even
the holiday crowds of France and Italy seem cold and con-
ventional compared with those of Austria.   The difference
is as great as that
between Strauss'
waltzes and those
of other compos-
ers.   Listen to a
fine rendering of
the waltz king's
" Beautiful Blue
Danube," "Wine,
W o m e n,   a n d
Song," and "Art-
ist's Life," and
you will find your
pulse beating in
unison with that
of the great heart
of the Austrian
Empire.

THE TEMPLE OF THESEUS IN THE
VOLKSGARTEN.

MAXIMILIAN PLATZ.

Well-dressed civilians, handsome officers, and pretty Viennese ladies here form a charming picture that quickens the pulse, and makes one feel good-natured toward the world. The scene is that of southern merriment and vivacity, and every one appears to be without a trace of care or sadness.

At such a time we cannot wonder that the Viennese say enthusiastically of their loved capital: "*Es giebt nur eine Kaiserstadt; es giebt nur ein Wien!*" — "There's only one imperial city; there's only one Vienna!"

Yet, as even through the melodies of Strauss

THE STATUE OF THESEUS.

there often runs a minor strain of sadness, so in the midst of all this merriment a face is sometimes seen which seems to be at variance with its surroundings. One night, as I was seated in Vienna's City Park, I perceived at a table near me a party of Americans. I recognized them all without surprise, save a young lady whom I assuredly should not have known apart from her companions; for when I had last seen her, fifteen years before, she was a little child. Her subsequent history, however, had been known to me, as one of the kind that wrecks life's happiness irretrievably, and rolls upon the sepulchre of buried hopes a massive stone. I sat and watched her altered face, while the wild, passionate music

SCHWARTZENBERG PARK.

rose and fell, and, as I did so, realized sadly that the joyous
girl whom I had known was dead. I could remember her as
a sensitive, impressionable little creature, so close to Nature's
heart that she loved and was tender to everything living,
even to grass and mosses; and, in her happy innocence of
evil, feared nothing on the earth, or under it, or above it.
She was a plump, dimpled child, — with the pink and white
of the flowers in her cheeks, and the brown and gold of
autumn leaves in her flying curls and shining eyes, and the
notes of the birds in her childish voice, as it rippled all day
long in mirth and glee. There was the freedom of the wind
in the quick movements of her tireless feet and nimble hands,
and the sunshine of God was in her gladsome face, as round
and shining then as a miniature sun. She loved to tell me

of the fairies who slid down the moonbeams at night to visit her, swung on the spider-webs, lurked in the flower-bells, showed her their banquet halls, and told her all their secrets.

But, at last, the beautiful transparent shell of innocence and

A CONCERT HALL.

trust, in which she had lived for nearly twenty years, was rudely shattered at a blow, and she was suddenly thrust out from her child's paradise into the cruel maelstrom of the world; and on the day of that catastrophe, the little girl, whom I had known, had died, and the sad-featured woman whom I saw before me in

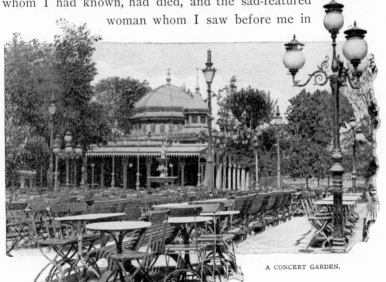

A CONCERT GARDEN.

the garden had been born. I could see plainly, from where
I sat, that the wings on which her hopes and high ideals had
soared had become, like those of a wounded butterfly, torn and

THE MUSIC-HALL, CITY PARK.

broken by the rough touch of life; that her illusions had fled;
that the flowers of love had become scentless and artificial, and
that even the sunshine was a scorching flame. It was evident
that the remainder of the way through life seemed to her
long and hard; for her feet were already weary; the dust
of earth and falling tears had dimmed her aching eyes, and
the song that used to pour forth from her throat, like the
trill of a bird, was stilled forever. The realization of all
this, and of the tragic undertone of life of which she was
the exponent, made even Strauss' music that night unendur-
able; and, unperceived by the sad woman who had replaced

the happy child whom I had known, I left the park and walked alone beneath the stars.

One must not think of Vienna as being exclusively devoted to amusement; for, in the number and value of its libraries and art collections, it stands in the first rank among the cities of the world. Thus its Imperial Library contains more than four hundred and ten thousand volumes, that of the University one hundred and ten thousand, the Emperor's private collection fifty thousand, Prince Lichtenstein's fifty thousand, and about a dozen other libraries have from twenty to fifty thousand volumes each. The collections of engravings in Vienna are unsurpassed, — the Imperial Library alone possessing nearly two hundred thousand, while those of Prince Esterhazy

THE HEROES' SQUARE.

and the Archduke Charles would, if combined, exceed that number. The picture galleries of Vienna are, also, of great value, numbering in the aggregate nearly six thousand paintings, and all these collections are open to the public, free of charge.

From the Ringstrasse, at one point, a massive portal known as the Palace Gate, leads to a spacious area called the Heroes' Square. The name is comprehended at a glance, when the visitor perceives the two equestrian statues which, from the ends of the enclosure, seem to be charging upon each other like knights in a mediæval tournament. One of them represents the Archduke Charles, the ablest general of Austria in the early

THE STATUE OF THE ARCHDUKE CHARLES.

part of this century; who, had he not been pitted against such a won-

derful antagonist as Napoleon, would have acquired even greater military fame than has been accorded him. The statue portrays him waving exultantly the Austrian flag on the battle-field of Aspern, where, on the 21st of May, 1809, a temporary check was given by his troops to the French army. The other statue, in this area, is that of Prince Eugène, one of the most distinguished generals and statesmen of

THE STATUE OF PRINCE EUGÈNE.

the eighteenth century, and one of the most interesting figures in history.

The story of his life reads like a romance. Born in Paris, and being a relative of the powerful Cardinal Mazarin, his talents would have been devoted to his native land but for a mortal affront given by Louis XIV., who, sneering at his insignificant personal appearance, refused him a commission in the army. The young man vowed he would never again set foot upon French soil, save as an en- emy, and that the King should some day bitterly repent his conduct. Ac- cordingly, leav- ing France, he offered his services to the Emperor of Austria, and was ac- cepted. Here he soon demonstrated that he

THE BELVEDERE PALACE.

had military talents of the highest order. Only eight years after the royal insult offered him in Paris, he com- manded the Austrian army against the French, and six years later, in 1697, gained a decisive victory over the Turks. In 1701 he again fought successfully against his native land, and captured the French marshal who opposed him. Alive now to his great abilities, Louis XIV. offered Eugène a marshal's staff, if he would return and enter the French army. It was a proud moment for the Austrian commander when he received the offer and — declined it. In 1704, in coöperation with the Duke of Marlborough, he again defeated the French in the great battle of Blenheim, and during the following year expelled the French from Italy. Moreover, these campaigns were followed, ten years later, by his brilliant victories over the Turks, by means of

which he regained for Austria much disputed territory, especially the important city of Belgrade, now the capital of Servia. With such a record as a warrior, to which was added an illustrious career as a statesman, it is not strange that he became a favorite with

THE VESTIBULE OF THE BELVEDERE PALACE.

the Austrian Court, and the idol of the people. His residence in Vienna, given him by the Emperor, was the Belvedere Palace, which, till quite recently, contained one of the finest picture galleries in Europe; but these art treasures have now been removed to the Imperial Museum on the Ringstrasse.

Behind the Heroes' Square stands the Imperial Palace, which is not so much one enormous edifice as a collection of buildings that has been gradually growing and adding to itself for about six hundred years. So many interesting historical associations are, therefore, connected with this home of the imperial family that the Viennese have been reluctant to replace it by a modern structure; but it has at last been decided to do so, and an immense addition is now in process of construction, the cost of which is estimated at twenty million dollars. It must not be supposed that the imperial family reserves for its

THE INNER GATE OF THE IMPERIAL PALACE.

sole use the whole of this palace. The greater part of it has long been a museum, in which are three departments of great value. The first is the Imperial Library, in the long halls of which, in addition to the four hundred thousand books already mentioned, are twenty thousand precious manuscripts and twelve thousand volumes of music. The second is a rare and beautiful collection of ancient bronzes, cameos,

THE HERCULES STATUES AT THE PALACE ENTRANCE.

and coins, among which one could spend with pleasure several hours; and the third is the Imperial Treasury, where the visitor beholds the renowned State jewels of the empire, resplendent in the crowns of both the Emperor and Empress, and, also, countless objects of historic value, such as Napoleon's crown and coronation robe as King of Italy; the cradle of his little son, inlaid with pearl and gold; the sceptre, sword, and crown of Charlemagne; and, among other gems, the famous diamond of Charles of Burgundy, which weighs one hundred and thirty

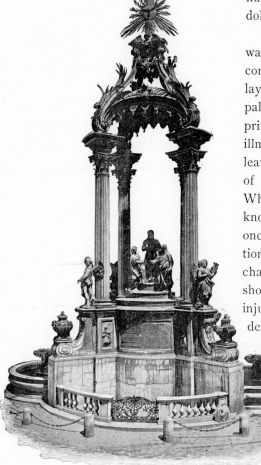

carats, and is valued at two hundred and eighty thousand dollars.

In 1805, when Napoleon was bombarding Vienna to compel its surrender, there lay in an apartment of this palace a young Austrian princess who, on account of illness, had been unable to leave the city with the rest of the imperial household. When this fact was made known to Napoleon, he at once ordered that the direction of the guns should be changed, and that great care should be exercised to avoid injuring the imperial residence. Little did he imagine that the young lady, whose life he perhaps thus saved, would a few years later be-

A VIENNESE FOUNTAIN.

THE MUSEUM AND MONUMENT.

A COURTYARD OF THE PALACE, AND STATUE OF JOSEPH II.

come his wife, and, as Marie Louise, Empress of France, take the place of his discarded Josephine.

In a little square, adjoining the Imperial Palace, stands the bronze equestrian statue of another famous sovereign of Austria, — Joseph II., son of Maria Theresa. Few men have been actuated by nobler motives than he, and few have been more cruelly disappointed in the execution of their plans. In Joseph's case the difficulty lay in the fact that he was in advance of his time. All the great reforms which he endeavored to inaugurate, such as the emancipation of the serfs, religious freedom, reduction of taxation, met with relentless opposition from both his clergy and nobility, and the Hungarian magnates openly threatened insurrection. Accordingly, in 1790, Joseph found himself compelled to revoke his proposed reforms, and confess that his noble aspirations and endeavors had ended in disastrous failure. Always delicate in health, he never recovered from the blow, and, in a few weeks, sank into an untimely grave. The lives of few European sovereigns present a more interesting study than that

of Joseph II. In the performance of his public duties he worked
as hard as Frederick the Great, whom, though the enemy of
Austria, he greatly admired. In summer he usually rose at five,
and in winter at six. Then, slipping on a dressing-gown, he
would attend to his accumulated despatches until nine o'clock,
when he stopped for a frugal breakfast. He then dressed and
went to the audience-chamber. Here he was not only accessible to all, but, being well-acquainted with the tyranny of Court
underlings, he used to go at regular intervals into the corridor,
outside his audience-room, to personally ascertain if any one who
wished to see him had been refused admission. He is said to
have never kept any one waiting with whom he had made
an appointment. At about twelve he would conclude his audi-
ences, and go   to the park, where he himself
usually drove in   an open carriage drawn by two
horses. The   drive finished, Joseph returned

ST. CHARLES' CHURCH.

THE AUGUSTA BRIDGE AND
RUDOLPH BARRACKS.

for dinner, which was brought to his apartment in five deep dishes, placed one upon the other. These were laid on the stove to be kept warm until the Emperor was ready; for, on returning from his drive, he often forgot his noon repast while looking over the important despatches that had arrived during his absence. His life was exceptionally lonely, for his independent, democratic spirit met with such opposition that he found among the aristocracy at times more enemies than friends. When an Austrian noble, one day, hinted that it would be more suitable for him to associate with his equals, rather than with people of no birth at all, like Mozart, for example, who was "merely a musician," Joseph retorted, "If I wished to keep company with only my equals, I should be obliged to go down to the vault of the Capuchins, and pass my time among the coffins of my ancestors."

It is an interesting fact that near the field of Austerlitz — where Napoleon, in 1805, gained over Austria and Russia one of his most brilliant victories — a monument has been erected to commemorate an event of a very different nature from that of the great conflict. Thirty-six years before that battle Joseph II., while riding through the country, saw an aged peasant leaning exhausted on his plow, unable to complete his work. Touched by the sight, the Emperor immediately dismounted and, putting his hands to the plow, finished the old man's task for him. The monument, which serves as a memorial of this imperial act, is surmounted by the Austrian eagle, and on the pedestal is depicted, in relief, the figure of Joseph II. holding the plow, while his astonished servant stands waiting near by, with the Emperor's horse.

Saint Stephen's Cathedral occupies so central a position in Vienna that streets are numbered from it in

ST. STEPHEN'S CATHEDRAL.

all directions, much as distances were reckoned from the Golden
Milestone in the Roman Forum. Its graceful spire, four hundred
and fifty feet in height, is the dominating feature of the land-
scape at a considerable distance from the city; while, upon
close approach, it still remains an object of great beauty —
tapering gradually from base to summit, and covered all the
way with artistic stone-
carving and Gothic or-
namentation. So
straight does it
appear that I
could scarcely
believe the
statement
that its apex
leans toward
the North,
with a devia-
tion from the
perpendicular of
more than three feet.
On several occasions, its
lofty belfry has served as a
place of anxious observa-

ONE OF THE OLD RAMPARTS.

tion, when the fate of the Austrian capital seemed trembling in the balance. Here, for example, two hundred
years ago the Viennese officials stood to watch the movements of the Turks, who, two hundred thousand strong,
had invested the city in the form of a crescent; and, while
offering peace and protection to those who would surrender,
swore by the beard of the Prophet that, if obliged to take
the capital by force, they would spare no one, but would
kill every man and carry into captivity all the women and
children. Here, also, on the sixtieth day of the siege, those

eager watchers discerned with joy the banners of the approaching Polish army, which, led by Sobieski, was hastening
to their rescue.   The principal bell in the church tower
commemorates this victory of the Cross over the Cres-

INTERIOR OF ST. STEPHEN'S.

cent, since it was
cast from the
bronze of one
hundred and
eighty cannon
taken on that
occasion from the
Moslems. Here,
too, is the enor-
mous crescent
which the Vien-
nese authorities
fastened to the
spire, in order
to induce the
Turks to spare
the sacred edifice

through fear of injuring the emblem of their faith. From
this tower one can look out upon the roof and see there,
outlined by a multitude of colored tiles, a monster eagle
with extended pinions, probably the largest figure of a
bird in the world. At all events, the distance from the tip
of one wing to the extremity of the other is one hundred
and eighty feet, and each eye is composed of four large
gilded tiles.

Saint Stephen's is, unquestionably, one of the grandest
temples ever reared for Christian worship, and few cathedrals
in the world have left upon my mind such ineffaceable impressions of sublimity. I love to stand by one of its huge pillars
in the twilight and silently absorb its solemn grandeur. At

THE ACADEMY OF THE FINE ARTS.

such a time the distant roof is lost in darkness, and the majestic columns rise into the gloom, like stately palms or tropic plants whose leaves and flowers are the delicately chiseled canopies, pinnacles, and statues that cling to the colossal shafts with countless filaments of stone.

As the interior stretches away into sombre immensity, the figures on these columns, half discerned and half divined, seem like the ghosts of former worshipers who, in past centuries,

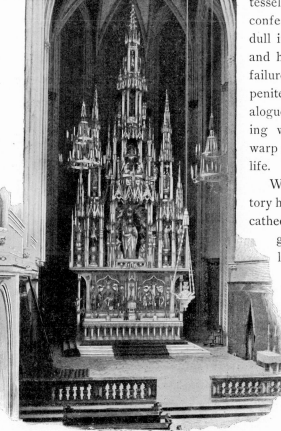

A HISTORIC ALTAR.

have knelt upon this tessellated pavement, and confessed to ears, now dull in death, their loves and hates, triumphs and failures, passions and penitence, — the long catalogue of sin and suffering which make up the warp and woof of human life.

What an eventful history has this old Viennese cathedral! Before the great High Altar — lost in the gloom and distance, save for the sanctuary lamp which glows in mid-air like a monster ruby — hundreds of mailèd soldiers of the Cross have knelt to receive the sacrament of con-

secration, ere they marched eastward to the Holy Land to rescue
from Moslem hands the sepulchre of Christ; and here, too, some
of these heroes, fallen in the conflict, have been brought again,
their steel-gloved hands still folded, as if in prayer, but this time
lying in eternal rest upon the sheathèd sword and pulseless heart.

Lingering one evening in this ancient sanctuary, I seemed
to see — where the faint light of dying day came stealing
through the lofty transept — the spectral standards carried
through these aisles by valiant knights of long ago; and even
to hear the distant echo of the clank of armor, and the clang
of lance and shield, together with the shouts of triumph,
hymns of praise, the wail of sorrow, and the *miserere* of despair,
all of which   have, in turn, for centuries been heard within these walls.

What sameness, yet
what infinite variety, there
is in this cathedral's life!
Before that altar has been
reared the stately cata-
falque, upon which Aus-
tria's imperial dead have
lain in solemn state, to be
replaced, it may be, the
next day by the plain bier,
whereon some weary child
of toil has found his first repose. To-day,
perhaps, the
mournful gran-
deur of the re-
quiem yields
to the joyous
splendor of
the nuptial

THE PULPIT OF ST. STEPHEN'S.

A PRINCELY RESIDENCE.

mass, — where bright eyes and resplendent gems relieve the sombre shadows of the church with the warm glow of youth and radiance of love; and these again to-morrow may give place to some display of gorgeous vestments, flashing in the light of countless tapers, when a distinguished prelate shall be consecrated, or one of Austria's sovereigns be crowned.

Perhaps the most impressive hour in St. Stephen's is that of the vesper service. The vast interior is then filled with reverent worshipers, whose whispered prayers float among the arches like the south wind sighing through the trees. Meantime, as taper after taper on the altar trembles into flame, like stars upon the darkening curtain of the night, the chancel becomes radiant with light, dimmed only by the smoke from censers swung by white-robed acolytes, while the officiating priests, in their rich vestments, appear the counterparts of figures in the stained-glass windows, glorious with varied colors. At length there comes a solemn pause; a silver-throated bell sends forth its thrice-repeated call, and then, before the hushed and kneeling multitude, the celebrant elevates the Host for adoration. A moment more, and, with a burst of harmony which rolls in a resistless flood from marble floor to vaulted roof, filling the chapels, aisles, and galleries with a tumultuous sea of sound, the congregation, priests, and choir join in a solemn symphony of praise.

A STREET CAR STATION.

Various features of street life in Vienna soon attract the tourist's attention. There is, for example, here, as in many other German cities, a system of service which is much cheaper and more accessible to the general public than that of our "District Telegraph Messengers," since at the various street corners are stationed no fewer than one thousand six hundred licensed *dienstmänner*, or porters, who will go on errands, and carry letters or parcels at the very reasonable rates established by law.

I observed with pleasure, also, the pretty little stations, where people awaiting horse-cars are protected from the weather. These are improvements; but on the other hand, one sees occasionally in the Austrian capital an evidence of conservatism which seems incredibly "behind the times." Thus, we were greatly amused by the Viennese mode of sprinkling the

WATERING THE STREETS.

streets. The water-cart was somewhat like our own, but in the rear of it protruded a piece of hose, about three feet in length, resembling an elephant's tail. This curious appendage was held by a man who walked behind the cart, like a page supporting a lady's train, and it was the duty of the wretched individual (whose rubber apron by no means prevented him from being drenched), to swing the hose violently right and left, scattering the water over as much of the street as possible. The sight of this ridiculous combination of discomfort and unnecessary physical exertion never failed to excite our laughter.

Looking from my window, one morning, I could have fancied that a multitude of monstrous mushrooms had sprung up from the pavement in a single night; for one of the migratory markets, characteristic of old European cities, had established itself here for the day, and I was looking down upon a mass of white umbrellas of enormous size, designed to shelter from the sun and rain provisions and proprietors alike. The market-women of Vienna, who thus sell their wares, are notorious for their volubility

WHITE UMBRELLAS.

and the vituperative power of their tongues. One of the escapades of Joseph II., when a young man, was to go among them in disguise, and overturn a basket of eggs, or play some similar prank, that he might listen to their torrents of abuse; in return for which, however, he was always willing to pay well for the mischief he had done.

One of the most important business streets in Vienna is the Graben, which, as the name denotes, was once a part of the moat outside the fortifications; and, strange as it may seem to the tourist of the present time, many of the attractive

shops that tempt him here, to-day, stand on the site of the
old city battlements.   Among the modern buildings which
adorn the Graben is a singular relic of the past, well worth
inspection.   It is the stump of an old tree, securely fastened
to the wall by an iron band.   It is called the "*Stock im
Eisen*," or the "Iron Stick," from the fact that it is com-

pletely covered
with nails that
have been driven
into it in accord-
ance with an an-
cient custom, the
significance   of
which   is   un-
known.   Its ap-
pearance, there-
fore, is precisely
that of an iron
club.   That this
old tree, which
apparently could
not crumble now

THE "STOCK IM EISEN."

if it should try, was formerly looked upon as sacred, there
can be no doubt; and it is said to have once marked the
terminus of the great Weiner Wald, or Forest of Vienna,
which then extended to this moat.

In the centre of the Graben stands an architectural mon-
strosity, sadly at variance with the handsome shops along
the street.   It is, I think, without exception the ugliest
monument in the world.   It is entitled the Trinity Column;
but what that theological doctrine has to do with its con-
fused array of clouds, men, angels, animals, and devils is
difficult to understand.   At the first glance, it seemed to me the
petrified result of an explosion of dynamite beneath the monkey

THE GRABEN AND ST. STEPHEN'S SPIRE.

cage of a menagerie; and as it was erected, in 1679, to commemorate the cessation of the plague in Vienna, one almost regrets that the architect, at least, did not succumb to the epidemic.

Until about two hundred years ago, the sovereigns of Austria were buried in the crypt of St. Stephen's Cathedral. Since then, however, their bodies have been laid to rest in the vault of the far humbler Church of the Capuchins. Guided by one of the brothers, I descended into this sub-terranean chamber of the royal dead. The faint light from the monk's lamp flickered fitfully upon the dark stone pave-ment and the bronze sarcophagi which lie here side by side; and, halting before each, the priest would strike the metal cover with his key and speak the name of its dead occupant. The largest and most elaborate of these contains the remains of Maria Theresa. Near that are the coffins of her husband, Francis I., and her son, Joseph II.; a few steps further one per- ceives the tomb of Marie

THE CHURCH OF THE CAPUCHINS.

Louise, the second wife of Napoleon, beside which lies the casket of her son, who was called by his imperial father the King of Rome, but is named here by the title given him in Austria, the Duke of Reichstadt. Another tomb in this crypt is that of the Archduke Maximilian, Emperor of Mexico; who, lured by the glitter of a phantom crown, was induced to leave his exalted position in Austria, to found a short-lived empire on the shores of the New World, and met an

THE CRYPT OF THE CAPUCHINS.

ignominious death at the hands of those who refused to submit to a foreign dictator. The most recent member of the imperial family buried here was the unfortunate Prince Rudolph, son of the present Emperor, and heir-apparent to the throne, the mystery of whose tragic death, in 1889, has never been openly explained. His afflicted father, Francis Joseph, on the day of the tragedy, sent to the Pope the following pathetic telegram: "Holy Father," he wrote, "please decide whether my poor boy is to have Christian burial or not, exactly like any other man. I ask for no favor. As for myself, I am resolved to abdicate." I saw a wreath of flowers lying upon Rudolph's coffin, and the ribbon attached to it, in token of his wife's affection, bore the three words, "From thy Stephanie."

PRINCE RUDOLPH.

Allusion has been made to the effect which the death of her husband produced on Maria Theresa. The end had come so suddenly that he had been incapable of receiving the last sacrament. The Empress, therefore, felt it her duty to offer up constant prayers for the repose of his soul, and frequently went down, for this purpose, to his tomb in the gloomy vault of the Capuchins. Toward the last of her life, her health became so impaired that she had to be lowered into the crypt in a chair. On the last of these mournful visits, as the Empress was being drawn up, the rope broke, and she exclaimed: "He wants to keep me with him. Well, I shall come soon." Unfortunately, in her devotion to her husband's memory, Maria Theresa compelled others to do unwillingly what was to her a duty and a consolation. Thus, in 1769, her beautiful daugh-

THE PRINCESS STEPHANIE.

ter, Maria Josepha, was betrothed to King Ferdinand IV. of Naples.   Before setting out for her new home, Maria Theresa ordered her to descend into the sepulchral vault and offer up a prayer beside the coffin of her father. The young girl implored to be excused from this appalling duty, but her mother was inexorable, and the unfortunate Josepha, trembling with fear, was led down into the crypt.   Scarcely four months had elapsed since the corpse of her sister-in-law had been buried there, and the small-pox, which caused her death, had been so virulent as to render it impossible to embalm the body.   The noxious odor was still perceptible, and the fetid air communicated the infection.   Accordingly, soon after her visit to the vault, the young Archduchess was seized with small-pox and died on the very day appointed for her departure to Naples.

THE OBELISK.

One of the finest works of art in the Austrian capital is the tomb of the Archduchess Christina, daughter of Maria Theresa, in the Church of the Augustines. It is a product of Canova's genius, and the sculptor's own tomb, in the Church of the Frari in Venice, was modeled after this; as if no

TOMB OF THE ARCHDUCHESS CHRISTINA.

finer idea could be expressed, and no more perfect work could be executed. The monument is in the form of a marble pyramid, approached by a flight of steps. The door of the sepulchre in the centre of the pyramid is slightly ajar, and toward this a number of marble figures appear to be slowly moving. This is not an exaggerated statement; for, after watching these wonderfully life-like statues till the mind fully comprehends the motive of the work, it is easy to imagine them endowed with life, and one half expects to see them disappear within the open portal. They represent a group of mourners, and typify qualities for which the Archduchess was distinguished. The principal figure, carrying in an urn the ashes of the deceased, symbolizes Virtue, and is attended by two maidens, bearing torches to illumine, and flowers to relieve, the gloom and sadness of the tomb.

Another beautiful statue typifies Benevolence, and supports a feeble, decrepit man symbolizing Old Age. Childhood is also

THE WIEN.

represented, mourning its benefactress, by a youthful figure, whose folded hands and drooping head indicate that in this bereavement children, too, have cause for grief.

Beside the entrance to the tomb is a recumbent lion guarding the ducal sepulchre, and against this leans the Genius of Death with inverted torch. Over the doorway is a medallion of the Archduchess, and beneath it, in the concise Latin, are three words, which in the presence of these sculptured forms are sufficient and appropriate. They are *"Uxori optimae Albertus,"* — "Albert to his perfect Wife."

Many travelers come to Vienna, expecting to find it situated actually on the banks of the "Beautiful, blue Dan-

THE ELIZABETH BRIDGE AND ST. CHARLES' CHURCH.

ube." In reality, however, the great river of Austria is two miles away. Nevertheless, to all intents and purposes Vienna does lie on the Danube, for it is connected with it by a navigable canal. At one point this " Little Danube," as it is called, forms a junction with the river Wien, which, although still more insignificant in size, gives the German name Wien, and the English Vienna, to the Austrian capital. The pointed strip of land, at which this union is effected, advances into their commingled waters like the prow of a wherry. The river Wien, like the Manzanares at Madrid, frequently runs dry ; yet, like its Spanish rival also, it is capable of assuming threatening dimensions, when swollen by copious rains or melting snow. In summer, however, the appearance of

THE JUNCTION OF THE WIEN AND THE CANAL.

massive bridges spanning a dry and stony cañon provokes a smile until the occasional necessity for them is explained.

Strolling one day beside this river, we saw an illustration of the fact that whatever the Germans attempt to do, they usually do with thoroughness. They wished, for example, in this instance, to commemorate a certain name, and we in consequence perceived before us " Schwarzenberg Street " and " Schwarzenberg Bridge," " Schwarzenberg Palace," also, in the distance, " Schwarzenberg Park " beyond

it, and, in the foreground of them all, the equestrian statue
of Schwarzenberg himself. "Who, then, is this Schwarzenberg?" we naturally inquired, as, led by the continual repe-
tition of his name, we drew still nearer to the figure of this
mounted warrior.   But as soon as we read the inscription
on the pedestal, we recollected, of course, that Schwarzenberg was the general who, in 1814, led the Austrian army

THE STATUE OF SCHWARZENBERG.

in the allied
host that finally
crushed Napo-
leon.

Alas for poor
humanity! The
leveling of Vi-
enna's fortifica-
tions, and their
transformation
into pleasure-
grounds and
stately prome-
nades, have not
been equivalent
to the beating
of swords into
plowshares, nor

has the capital's embellishment inaugurated a millennium of
peace.   The defeats which Austria experienced at the hands
of Prussia at Königgrätz and Sadowa, in 1867, have not
lessened, but increased, the military spirit of the nation, and
Vienna's line of fortifications has merely been expanded into
a larger circle.   In fact, some of the most conspicuous
buildings in and near the city are barracks; and the Imperial
Arsenal of Vienna is one of the largest structures in the
world.   This building is visible at a great distance, and looks

THE ARSENAL.

like a section of a walled city, — since it is more than a third of a mile in length and a quarter of a mile in breadth. Within this vast enclosure are barracks, gun factories, a cannon foundry, and a military museum. The latter is especially interesting from the number of personal relics it contains of Austrian warriors, such as Wallenstein's written orders to General Pappenheim, found soaked in blood on his lifeless body after the battle of Lützen; the hat of Marshal Aldringen, pierced by bullets; the hat of General Heister, which was pinned to his head by an arrow at the siege of Vienna, in 1683;

THE ENTRANCE TO THE ARSENAL.

the sword of Napoleon's old antagonist, General Wurmser; the uniform and a lock of hair of the brave Prince Eugène, together with many memorials of Joseph II., Marshal Schwarzenberg, and the Archduke Charles.

Strangely enough, in the midst of all these souvenirs of bloodshed and workshops for the enginery of war, there stands a little church, dedicated to the worship of the Prince of Peace! That the world is not yet ready to admit the practicability of Christ's noble precepts of universal brotherhood and non-resistance, is proved by the fact that the leading Christian nations are, to-day, armed to the teeth, grievously burdened with enormous standing armies and expensive navies, and actively engaged in appropriating to themselves the semi-civilized portions of the earth, on the absolutely anti-Christian theory that Might

THE FRANZ JOSEPH BARRACKS.

makes Right; while the first and most conspicuous result of having brought Japan into close contact with Christendom has been to transform her into one of the strongest naval powers in the world. The incongruity of building a church within this Arsenal is as great as that of inscribing on Prussian shells the legend, "*Gott mit uns.*" Yet, there can be no doubt that the teaching of Jesus represents the ideal

THE GATEWAY TO THE BARRACKS.

condition which His professed disciples should endeavor
to realize, instead of diametrically opposing it; and the
words of the poet are still true, if not convincing, when he
sings:

ENTRANCE TO PRATER.

"Were half the power that fills the world with terror,
    Were half the wealth bestowed on camps and courts,
  Given to redeem the human mind from error,
    There were no need of arsenals or forts."

Of all the pleasure-grounds enjoyed by the Viennese, the largest is the immense park called the Prater, which is more than three miles in length, and has an area of four thousand acres. Up to the time of Joseph II. this was a royal game-preserve, well stocked with deer; but that liberal monarch gave it to the people for a pleasure-resort, and as such it has ever since remained. Moreover, as if the enormous areas of the Prater and the various

A CAFÉ IN THE PRATER.

city parks were not sufficient, several extensive private gardens, such as those of Prince Schwarzenberg, of the Lichtenstein family, and of the

IN THE PRATER.

Belvedere Palace, are thrown open to the public daily, after
the fashion of the villas near Rome; nor does such generosity
seem to be abused as in some other countries, where those
to whom such privi- leges are extended frequently act as if the property were theirs,
and ruthlessly pick flowers, trample on
the lawns, and devastate the shrubbery.

It is a never-to- be-forgotten experience to view the Prater on a pleasant summer even- ing or a holiday.
Thousands of peo- ple are then either
riding along the spa- cious driveways,
strolling among the trees (many of

A SWEEPER IN THE PRATER.

them brilliantly illuminated), or seated in the numerous concert gardens, listening to those strains of music which seem
almost as necessary to the existence of the Viennese as the
air they breathe. It was at such a time that, on a scrap of
paper, in the midst of innocent merriment and delightful
music, in this park, the following lines were traced:

TO–DAY

"The sun will set at day's decline."
  Qu'importe?
Quaff off, meanwhile, life's sparkling wine.
Of what avail are timorous fears,
Foreboding sighs and idle tears?
They hinder not the hurrying years.
  Buvons!

"This fleeting hour will soon be past."
  Qu'importe?
Enrich its moments while they last.
To-day is ours. Be ours its joy.
Let not to-morrow's cares annoy.
Enough the present to employ.
  Vivons!

"These pleasures will not come again."
       Qu'importe?
Enjoy their keenest transport, then.
If but of these we are secure,
Be of their sweetness doubly sure,
That long their memory may endure.
       Rions!

"With time, love's ardor always cools."
       Qu'importe?
Leave that lugubrious chant to fools.
Must doubt destroy our present bliss?
Shall we, through fear, love's rapture miss,
Or lose the honey of its kiss?
       Aimons!

"The sun will set at day's decline."
       Qu'importe?
Will not the eternal stars still shine?
So even in life's most dreary night
A thousand quenchless suns are bright,
Blest souvenirs of past delight.
       Allons!

THE PRATER.

To those who have studied popular gatherings in different lands, the contrast between the North and South of Europe is remarkable. The difference seems to depend largely on the amount of alcohol imbibed. This steadily diminishes as one goes southward, and in Austria the almost universal beverage is the light and wholesome Vienna beer.

SCHÖNBRUNN.

Hence we discerned here practically no intoxication, and the happiness and good behavior of a Viennese crowd are proverbial.

The favorite summer residence of the imperial family of Austria is Schönbrunn, situated a few miles distant from the capital. I shall never forget the beautiful spring day when I first visited this Austrian Versailles. Its luxuriant park was at its loveliest; the esplanade was soft with turf and bright with flowers; and, outlined on the sides, against great walls of carefully trimmed foliage, numerous marble statues were so cunningly displayed, that we could almost fancy them the natural inhabitants of the place. At one point, on an elevation overlooking these extensive grounds, is a pretty gallery called the Gloriette. This was, in summer, a favor-

ite resort of the Empress Maria Theresa, who would retire
here with books, papers, and despatches and attend to affairs
of State in the open air, sentinels having been posted in the
vicinity to warn
off all intruders.

Both the park
and palace of
Schönbrunn are
thronged with
interesting mem-
ories. It was in
this garden, for
example, in 1809,
when Napoleon
had established
his headquarters
here, that he
narrowly es-
caped assassina-
tion. He had
just alighted

IN THE PARK OF SCHÖNBRUNN.

from his horse after a review, when a young German pushed
through the crowd and asked if he could speak to the
Emperor. Napoleon received him kindly, but could not
understand his imperfect French. While speaking, the
young man held his right hand under his coat so constantly
that General Rapp regarded him with suspicion. He was,
accordingly, arrested and found to be armed with a large
knife. Far from denying that he had intended to kill the
Emperor, he boasted of it, regretting nothing save his failure
to accomplish his design. Napoleon sent for the youth, and
questioned him. "Why did you wish to kill me?" he asked.
"Because you are the oppressor of Germany," was the
reply. "Why did you not wish to kill the Emperor Francis?"

SCHÖNBRUNN AND THE GLORIETTE.

continued Napoleon; "it was he who commenced the war." "He is only a cipher," replied the young man, "some one could replace him; but if you were killed, you would have no successor." "If I should pardon you, what would you do?" "You would make a great mistake," was the reply, "for I would try again to kill you." Napoleon, however, offered to pardon him, on the sole condition that he should confess sorrow for his crime; yet the youth persisted in regretting nothing but his ill-success. Accordingly, he was left to his fate and was shot. No doubt Napoleon received a host of congratulations upon his escape; but, after all, should he have been congratulated? If he had died then, he would have passed away at the very zenith of his power and glory. There would have been no divorce, no second marriage, no little King of Rome to die at Schönbrunn in captivity; no retreat from Moscow, no Waterloo, and no St. Helena. In the light of history, it is not strange that the ancients held that one of man's greatest misfortunes is not to know the proper time at which to leave the world.

THE GLORIETTE.

One of the most interesting and pathetic objects in the palace of Schönbrunn is the room in which Napoleon's son,

THE DUKE OF REICHSTADT.

then called the Duke of Reichstadt, died at the age of twenty-one; for, by a strange coincidence, this ill-fated Prince expired, not only in the same room, but in the very bed, which had been occupied by his imperial father when conqueror of Vienna.

It is well that we cannot foresee the future. "Call no man happy before his death." What, for example, would have been Napoleon's feelings, could he have here divined, not only his own miserable death, but also that the child, whom he so ardently desired, would one day die upon that very couch, dependent on the charity of Austria! When the little King of Rome was born, Napoleon was at the summit of his power and glory. The gods seemed then to have denied him nothing. Master of Europe, sovereign of the mightiest empire that had existed for centuries, he had apparently founded his dynasty, since he possessed the great desire of his life, —a son and heir. The child's inheritance of glory seemed incalculable, and Napoleon was so fond and proud of him, that only those who saw his happiness then could realize what his sufferings must have been at St. Helena, when his idolized boy had forever lost the

A ROOM IN THE PALACE OF SCHÖNBRUNN.

IN THE VOLKSGARTEN.

glorious career to which he had been born, and was, to all intents and purposes, a prisoner at the court of Austria. Meneval, the private secretary of Napoleon, who accompanied Marie Louise and the little King of Rome to Vienna, where he re-

THE GOBELIN ROOM AT SCHÖNBRUNN.

mained until the landing of Napoleon from Elba, describes his parting from Napoleon's son: "I went to take my leave of the young Prince and noticed, with regret, his serious and even melancholy appearance. He had lost his childish gaiety, which had been so charming, and did not come to meet me as usual, and even gave me no sign of recognition.

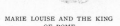

One might have said that misfortune was commencing to hover over that head which Providence seemed to have decorated with a crown, on his entry into life, in order to give a new example of the vanity of human greatness. He was like one of those victims which were led to sacrifice, adorned with flowers. Although he had been intrusted for more than six weeks to the persons in whose company I found him, he had not yet

MARIE LOUISE AND THE KING OF ROME.

become accustomed to them, and seemed

to look with distrust at the faces, which were still new to
him. I asked him, in their presence, if he would charge
me with any commission for his father, whom I was going
to see again. He looked at me sadly and significantly without answer-
ing ; then,
gently with-
drawing his
hand from
mine, he re-
tired into the
embrasure
of a window
some dis-
tance away.
After having
exchanged a
few words
with the per-
sons who
were in the

ARTIFICIAL RUINS AT SCHÖNBRUNN.

room, I approached the place where he was standing in
an attentive attitude. As I bent toward him to bid him
good-by, impressed by my emotion, he drew me toward the
window, and, looking at me with a touching expression,
said to me in a low voice, 'Monsieur Meva, you will tell
him that I still love him dearly.' The poor child felt even
then that he was no longer free, and that he was not
with his father's friends. When they ceased to call him
Napoleon, he was very indignant, and found the name of
Francis which was given him insignificant and ugly. I left
him in perfect health, and with a robust constitution that
promised a long life. He was also handsome, good and
endowed with lovable qualities which subsequently gained

for him the affection of his grandfather, the Emperor Francis."

But there are other souvenirs at Schönbrunn than those connected with Napoleon. On my first visit, in 1874, as I was standing near the obelisk in the park, I suddenly saw approaching me, on horseback, a lady beautiful of face and form, who rode her horse with perfect grace; and, marvelous to relate, was mother of the handsome Prince Rudolph, who rode beside her like a lover. The vision passed me like the wind, but not too rapidly for me to recognize the fact that I had seen one of the celebrated beauties of the world, — the Empress of Austria. In 1890 as I stood again within the shadow of that obelisk, or strolled about the pretty, artificial Roman ruins in these grounds, I thought with sadness of the changes which had taken place at Schönbrunn since that time; for now the Empress, a great invalid, lives chiefly on the distant Isle of Corfu in profound retirement, and the bright boy who rode so proudly at her side lies within the gloomy vault of Austria's imperial dead.

In the palace of Schönbrunn is another apartment of tragic interest to those who sympathize with Austria. It is the bedroom of the Emperor's brother, Maximilian, shot like

THE EMPRESS OF AUSTRIA.

a criminal in Mexico, — the dupe and victim of Napoleon III. His portrait hangs upon the wall, and near it is that of his wife, Carlotta. We saw, also, a sash embroidered by Carlotta's hands, which, when she said farewell to her husband, she tied about him, — over the uniform he was doomed to wear, at last, to execution. Yet, even at the worst, his fate was preferable to hers. Poor Carlotta, driven insane through hopeless grief! So generous and kind-hearted was Maximil-

THE BEDROOM OF MAXIMILIAN.

ian, that even the soldiers, who were ordered to shoot him, shed tears at his untimely death, and their commanding officer asked Maximilian to forgive him. "I have nothing to forgive," replied the Emperor, "for as a soldier, you are obliged to obey orders." Then, turning to the troops and pointing to his breast, he said, "Be so good as to aim here." A moment later his words were obeyed; but ere the volley was fired, he was heard to murmur, "Carlotta! Carlotta!" The name of the woman he loved was the last on the lips of Maximilian of Mexico.

In one of the halls at Schönbrunn we found an antidote to these melancholy souvenirs in the remarks of a young American tourist who was conducted with us through the palace. He was attended by a courier, who carefully translated for him

THE NEW PALACE GATE.

the explanations of the palace guide. A prominent picture here portrays the baptism of Marie Antoinette, and one of the

figures in the painting is that of the composer Mozart. "That is Mozart," translated the courier. "What!" cried the tourist in amazement, mistaking the name, "Moses! Moses here in Vienna! I hate to lug around this courier," he presently explained to me, "but I have to. At first I tried to play it alone, but it wouldn't go. I can't make head or tail out of this blamed language. When I was traveling by myself, I used to be carried by places where I wanted to stop, because I thought that the sign,

MAXIMILIAN.

'*Ausgang,*' in the station was the name of the town; and only after several such experiences did I finally learn that '*ausgang*' is the German for ' exit.' "

The pleasantest excursions in the vicinity of Vienna are to be made upon the Danube. In fact, the best way to approach Vienna from the west is to leave the railroad at Passau or Linz, and take a steamboat down the Danube to the Austrian capital. In any case, that portion of the river should not be omitted from the tourist's itinerary, or he will lose one of the most delightful experiences of European travel. The natural scenery of the Danube is far more beautiful than that of the Rhine. At times, environing mountains make the river look like some fair lake in Switzerland; at other points, advancing

CARLOTTA.

cliffs force it to rush on like a torrent in a cañon. At every turn, an unseen hand seems to have drawn aside a curtain and

revealed a new and ever-changing panorama, whose objects of attraction are splendid cities, ruined castles, stately palaces, and picturesque châteaux; varied by smiling villages, fertile valleys, imposing mountains, and black-bearded forests, all of which make a journey on these waters a continual series of surprises. Nor is the element of history wanting here. One of the ruins, towering above the Danube, is Dürrenstein, the crumbling battlements of which acquire an added interest when

A VIEW ON THE DANUBE.

we remember their peculiar history; for this, in 1192, was the prison-house of Richard, England's "lionhearted" king — the bravest of those princely warriors, who bore the standard of the Cross against the Saracens in Palestine. Yet, if we may believe the well-known legend, Richard was not forgotten in this mountain fastness.

Who does not recall the story of Blondel, the English monarch's favorite minstrel, who, having vainly sought him for many months, came here at last, and sang beneath these towers the verses of a song, composed partly by himself and partly by Richard? It was a test of the presence of his master which he had often made with beating heart, but hitherto without

WEITSNECK ON THE DANUBE.

success. Imagine then his joy, when, pausing in the refrain, he heard it taken up and finished by the royal captive. Learning thereby the place of his imprisonment, his faithful follower proclaimed it to the world, and soon the "lion-hearted" Richard was set free. Whatever truth we may, or may not, attach to this pretty legend, of Richard's imprisonment here for more than a year there is no question. Hence, when Napoleon, in the early part of the century, was riding along the Danube at this point, he looked upon the towers of Dürrenstein, and, reining in his horse, exclaimed: "Those were barbarous times. How different they are now! You have beheld kings and emperors in my power, but I exacted from them neither

DANUBIAN SCENERY.

ransom nor sacrifice of liberty. The world has seen how I have treated those whom I might have imprisoned." Who could have then imagined that the successful warrior who uttered these words was to experience at the hands of the English, on the rock of St. Helena, a captivity longer and far more desolate than that of their own sovereign in this Austrian fortress?

Few people, save those who have sailed upon the Danube,

realize that it is one of the noblest, as well as one of the most important, rivers in the world. The poet Ovid, exiled to its shores, declared that the Danube did not yield in grandeur even to the Nile. From its cradle in the Black Forest, to its grave in the Black Sea, it sweeps along in majesty for sixteen hundred miles; and, like a passing sovereign, receives *en route* the homage and support of sixty tributaries. It is not strange, therefore, that from the time when it was the northeastern frontier of the Roman Empire, down to the present day, its banks have been the scene of desperate conflicts; and its wooded shores have echoed in succession to a score of different languages, as conquerors of various nationalities have tried to make these lands their own.

THE IRON GATES ON THE DANUBE.

To a reflective mind, the surface of this river seems like a magic mirror, which, touched with but a breath of imagination, will reveal the shadowy hosts, whose bones have long since whitened in its dark blue depths. Inspired by such thoughts we almost hear the windings of this stream again reëcho to the bugles of the Roman cohorts, led by a Trajan or an Antonine; and see once more reflected in its waves the hosts of Attila; the hordes of southward-moving Goths; the long array of Christian pilgrims on their way to Palestine, the steel-clad warriors of the Cross; the invading armies of the Moslems, making these banks resound to the inspiring cry of "*Allah il Allah*"; and, finally, the victorious legions of Napoleon, — all of whom have, in turn, appeared to take possession of the Danube, yet who have, ultimately, passed away like shadows on its surface, while the grand river still rolls on,

HISTORIC SHORES.

as little altered by these would-be conquerors, as by the swallows that last summer flew from shore to shore. For Mother Earth heeds not those who claim that they possess her. How many has she heard boast that they owned her! But it is she who owns them all at last.

It is, however, when these lurid phantoms fade away, and in their place we see its waves reflect fair, cultivated fields and happy homes, that we behold the Danube at its best; for the same sun which once flashed here upon the spears of Roman legions, the crescent of the Moslems, the eagles of Napoleon, and, even recently, shone on the swords of warring Muscovites and Turks, now sheds its light on peaceful vil-

lages, reminding us anew of the great truth which Victor
Hugo grandly uttered when he wrote:

> " O toilers of the world, true glory lies
>   Not in great empires built o'er dead men's bones,
>   But in those deeds of charity and love
>   Which light our earth as Heaven is lit by stars."

CONSULTING BAEDECKER.

ST. PETERSBURG

ST PETERSBURG

NAPOLEON said, "Scratch a Russian, and you will find a Tartar." Fifty years later, Tourgénieff, one of the greatest writers Russia has produced, remarked: "The trouble with us Russians is that the Tartar is so close behind us. We are a semi-barbarous people still. We put Parisian kid gloves on our hands instead of washing them. At one moment we bow and utter polite phrases, and then go home and flog our servants."

THE TSAR.

THE TSARINA.

During the present century the empire of the Tsar has made enormous progress, but great bodies move slowly, and Russia is colossal. Russia has been compared to a giant sleeping under a shroud of snow. It occupies one-seventh of the entire land surface of our globe. The empire of Rome would have had to multiply itself four times to fill it. It could receive within its limits two such republics as the United States, including the mighty area of Alaska, and even then have room for Mexico, Great Britain, Germany, and France. In fact, the size of Russia, in one way, constitutes its weakness. Communication there is slow and difficult. The average population is but two inhabitants to the square mile. In Europe it is forty. The heterogeneous character of its people, too, is a disadvantage. If the Tsar wished to talk to all his subjects, he would have to speak

THE NORTHERN CAPITAL.

forty different languages or dialects. This being so, we can quite easily believe that both Napoleon and Tourgénieff were right; that Russia's cultivated people are few in number, and that her veneer of western civilization is still thin ; but give her as much time as older and more favored nations have enjoyed for their development, and possibly Russia may surpass them. Certain it is that in diplomacy, even now, she is a match for the rest of Europe. She holds a powerful position in the East. Her Trans-Siberian railroad almost touches the Pacific. She gains from China what she has so long desired, — an open, fortified harbor on her eastern coast. She has, moreover, boldly advanced to the Gates of India; and on the Bosphorus (no

doubt, in pay-
ment for conces-
sions made by
the Sultan), has
said to England
" No," and Eng-
land dared not
move to the as-
sistance of Ar-
menia. As for the
west of Europe,
by her consum-
mate coquetry

THE APPROACH TO ST. PETERSBURG.

with France, she has acquired a powerful ally, without, however, promising to do for France what France would certainly
perform for her.

If this mighty empire shall continue for a generation
longer to be guided thus, it will unquestionably become one
of the most powerful factors in the world's development.

A CANAL IN ST. PETERSBURG.

It is a mem-
orable moment in
the traveler's life
when he beholds,
rising before him,
like some strange
exhalation from
the deep, St. Pe-
tersburg, the city
of the Tsars. A
dome, radiant
with gold, shines
through the mists
of morning, like
the sun emerging

from the sea. "That," he exclaims, "must be St. Isaac's!"
But, at the same moment, he asks himself in great astonishment, "Why was a capital ever built in such a place as
this, almost within the Arctic Circle, and scarcely above the

level of the sea?"
Its very name sug-
gests the answer,
for it is named
after its creator
— Peter the Great
— who, bursting
through the bar-
riers that bound
him to the Ori-
ent, selected this
strange site, that
he might possess
a window, as he

THE STEAMBOAT LANDING

called it, through which to look out upon civilized Europe.
Yet, of all localities in which to found a capital, this was the
most extraordinary. True, it is the point where the majestic
river Neva pours its blue waters into the Gulf of Finland;
but what a shore! A miserable marsh, half under water,
without stones, clay, wood, or building material of any kind,
— such was the spot on which this mighty capital was to be
reared. The only persons found here were a few solitary
fishermen, struggling for bare subsistence, in a place so little
known as to be nameless. These peasants pointed out to
Peter an old tree, on which a mark gave warning of the
perilous height to which the waves would sometimes rise.
Peter replied by ordering them to cut the old tree down.

At first it is impossible to realize these facts, so massive
and substantial does everything connected with the water-
front appear, and one is liable to forget what a stupendous

CRONSTADT HARBOR.

undertaking this of Peter's was. The obstacles opposing him would have been insuperable to most men; but Peter was not easily dismayed. Were laborers needed? He summoned hither multitudes of Russians, Tartars, Cossacks, Fins, and even two thousand criminals destined for Siberia, and ordered them to go to work. Was he in jest? They had no tools. It mattered not. The iron task-master said "work," and work they must. They, therefore, dug the soil with sticks or with their hands; and carried the earth away in their caps and aprons.

As a result of this terrific energy, within the space of one short year there had arisen on these freezing marshes thirty thousand houses. Yet at what a cost! Beneath these buildings were the bones of nearly a hundred thousand wretched laborers, who, in those first twelve months from hunger and exposure, had perished in anguish and despair.

But that was nothing to the reckless Tsar. "One must break eggs," he said, "to make an omelet." Nevertheless, the inquiry is natural, "How did the Tsar persuade his subjects to reside in St. Petersburg, after the town was built?"

THE CITY OF THE TSARS.

Persuade! Peter used not persuasions, but commands. Were citizens needed? A word from him, and they came fast enough; for even this place was preferable to Siberia. Hundreds of merchants were forcibly transported here and ordered

"to take root." Mechanics and artisans were gathered together from the farthest corners of the vast empire and
brought here by thousands to swell the population and develop
the industries of the new imperial city. Many wealthy families
were required by an edict of the Tsar to take up their residence here, and to stay here in winter as well as summer.
Even the building of stone houses elsewhere in Russia was
forbidden, for stone houses and masons were wanted on the
Neva. They told him there were no stones with which to
build. No matter! Another edict from the Tsar was issued,
and thenceforth every boat that entered this harbor had to
bring a quantity of unhewn stones. St. Petersburg is, therefore, like the Pyramids, a most astounding specimen of autocratic power.

Filled with these thoughts, I never tired of looking at
the river Neva, apparently conquered and curbed by twenty
miles of granite quays. But is it really conquered? It still
looks dangerous. No portion of the city is more than fifteen

THE MOISKA QUAY.

feet above the ocean level, and hence it bears within its own breast the elements of its possible destruction. No skill can avoid occasional inundations. The Tsar can far more easily subdue the Nihilists than the Neva. This corner of the Gulf of Finland is so narrow that, when the west wind blows a gale, the water is heaped up into enormous billows, and should an ocean storm occur, just when the ice is disappearing in the spring, a catastrophe might happen, similar to that of 1824, when thirteen hundred houses

THE ST. NICHOLAS BRIDGE.

were destroyed and more than eight hundred persons were drowned. It is not beyond the range of possibility that this strange northern capital may some day disappear within the gloomy marshes from which it magically arose; for, viewed from any height, the whole stupendous mass seems to be floating unsteadily, like a huge vessel loaded to the water's edge with precious goods.

The enormous volume of its clear blue water makes the Neva one of the noblest rivers in Europe. Two hundred years ago, however, it was practically unknown. For centuries it had rolled through trackless forests, its shores resounding only to the shouts of savage fishermen. Now it is famed throughout the world and sweeps along in majesty to cast itself upon the bosom of the Baltic, and tell of the magnificence of the newborn city through which it has cleft its way.

A SHRINE FOR PRAYER.

Of course, with such a foundation as St. Petersburg possesses, it is emphatically a city of bridges, of which the finest bears the name of St. Nicholas. Beneath its iron arches and between its granite piers the river rushes on with rapid current, as if rejoicing to be free from icy fetters; for, during the greater part of the year, its waters are bridged by a crystal pavement — on which the heaviest burdens pass in safety — where large ships floated and blue waves tossed, perhaps, a fortnight before. The numerous branches of the Neva form, then, a series of glittering boulevards, into whose shining pavements lamp-posts are inserted, and which, for months, assume the characteristics of spacious, crowded thoroughfares, like white arms tightly locked about the city of the Tsar.

Near the extremity of this bridge stands a little structure which I at first supposed to be a toll-house. It is a shrine for prayer, containing a picture of St. Nicholas. I should be afraid to hazard a statement as to the number of such shrines in St. Petersburg. Their name is "legion." Before them, morning, noon, and night, there is the same show of devotion. No Russian, however busy he may be, will pass a church or the picture of a saint, without pausing long enough to cross himself. This is, indeed, a very common gesture in Russia; for every peasant, when he yawns, makes the sign of the cross before his mouth to prevent the devil from entering. Some even prostrate themselves before this

painting of St. Nicholas, and kiss the pavement. Be on
your guard, however, in such places; for pick-pockets com-
bine both business and religion here, and while they cross
themselves with one hand, they rob you with the other.

St. Isaac's Cathedral is an illustration of the fact that,
when she makes the effort, Russia can surpass the world
in the magnificence of her architecture; for the treasures
of her quarries are exhaustless, and the skill of her lapidaries is unexcelled. It is, however, unfortunate that there
is no eminence in St. Petersburg on which St. Isaac's could
have been placed; since, at even a little distance, it is impossible to see to advantage the stairways leading to its
various portals. Yet each of these steps is one gigantic
block of rose granite, worthy of the Egyptian temple of
Karnak; and every portico is supported by stupendous shafts
of the same material, sixty feet in height and seven feet in
diameter, and polished like the surface of a mirror.

ENTRANCE TO ST. ISAAC'S CATHEDRAL.

At first, however, the tourist may inquire: "What is there so remarkable in these porticos to distinguish them from others?" But, let him look along the columns for their lines of jointure. He will discover none, for each is a solid mass of beautifully polished stone. In fact, with the exception of Pompey's Pillar in Egypt, and the Alexander Column in St. Petersburg, they are the largest monoliths which the hand of man has ever quarried, turned, and polished. Ordinarily, one such entrance would suffice for any temple, but this magnificence is repeated on each of the four sides of St. Isaac's. We can, then, readily believe the statement that the whole cost of this cathedral exceeded fourteen million dollars, — one million having been expended in merely making a sufficiently strong foundation for the enormous mass. Moreover, like everything else in St. Petersburg, this is a proof of autocratic will, expressed in speed. Other cathedrals have been matured through centuries, but St. Isaac's was completed within forty years.

But if this be the exterior, how shall I describe the inte-

BRONZE DOORS OF ST. ISAAC'S.

ST. ISAAC'S CATHEDRAL.

rior of this temple of the North? Before its gilded altar-
screen are ten columns of malachite, thirty feet high, and
pillars of lapis-lazuli, each of which cost thirty thousand dollars. This exceeds every other display of these marvelous
stones that the world knows. We are accustomed to regard
a small fragment of either as a valuable ornament. Imagine,
then, whole columns of them five times as high as ourselves!

INTERIOR OF ST. ISAAC'S CATHEDRAL.

Yet this is only in keeping with the entire building; for in
St. Isaac's we tread a pavement of variegated marble; we
ascend steps of polished jasper; we clasp railings of pure
alabaster; and are surrounded by walls inlaid with verd-
antique and porphyry, interspersed with vast mosaic portraits of the saints, and shrines of gold incrusted with jewels.
One portrait of Christ is studded with diamonds, the largest
of which is valued at thirty-five thousand dollars. The whole,

in fact, is so magnificent as to appear incredible till actually
seen.

One of the first things to impress me in St. Petersburg
was the comparative lack of people in the streets.   Compared with London, Paris, and New York, it seems deserted.
The truth is, St. Petersburg is still too large for its
population.   Its buildings are too vast for the inhabitants.

THE NEVSKI PROSPEKT AND THE ADMIRALTY.

Its mammoth streets and squares
seem to have been designed for
the evolutions of large bodies of
troops.   On such a colossal scale is the
city built, that possibly the frame allotted to it
by its founder will never be adequately filled.   Moreover,
people die off rapidly in St. Petersburg.   Its death-rate
always exceeds its birth-rate.   The increase of its population
is largely dependent on arrivals from the country.   In Peter's
time there was danger from wild animals; and as late as
1714, two soldiers were devoured by them, while, in the same

year a woman was torn to pieces by wolves in front of Prince Menchikoff's house.

The characteristic Russian cab is unique. It has four wheels, each about as large as that of a wheelbarrow. Above them is raised a slender

MAMMOTH STREETS AND SQUARES.

framework, usually containing two seats: one for the driver, the other for the passenger. Under the circumstances, these seats are too near each other, since the proximity of the

A RUSSIAN DROSHKY.

driver's coat causes at times unpleasant zoölogical experiences. Of course there are some very elegant private droshkies, but

I am sure that the Deacon's "one-horse shay," in its last
moments, never had such a desperately seedy air as an ordinary Russian cab. An English nobleman once offered, it is
said, a thousand pounds to any one who would find, in a
civilized country, a more uncomfortable vehicle; but he has
his money still. By way of recompense, however, the horses
that draw even the poorest of these vehicles, are not such
skinny beasts as those which we commiserate in Paris and

THE NEVSKI PROSPEKT

Naples. Almost
without excep-
tion, Russian
horses, although
small, are swift,
elegantly formed,
and sleek. Their
harnesses are so
light that they
seem to be mere
ribbons of leath-
er; while a curi-
ous arch extends
from one shaft
to the other, mak-
ing the head of
the pretty animal
appear as if set in a picture-frame. These horses usually go
like the wind. No matter whether you are riding "by the
course" or "by the hour," you will be whirled over Peter's
paving-stones with a rapidity that startles you. Perhaps this
is owing to the fact that during the greater part of the year
these ponies draw light sleighs and sledges over an icy
crust, and thus become accustomed to a rapid gait.

The famous Alexander Column, in St. Petersburg, is a
monument of which all Russia may be justly proud. Even

A CHARACTERISTIC SCENE.

Egypt would have been satisfied with it. It is the greatest monolith of modern times, being a single column of red granite, eighty-four feet in height and fourteen in diameter, exclusive of pedestal and capital. When one beholds it standing so securely, it is hard to realize the immense amount of labor necessary to bring it from the mountain quarry and erect it here. But since the whole of St. Petersburg is built upon a swamp, it was necessary to drive into the soil six series of piles, one above the other, to form a sufficiently strong founda- tion for the enormous bur- den of four hundred tons resting on so small a base. Upon the pedestal of this column, which, like the capital, is of bronze, is the brief inscription, "Grateful Russia to Alexander I." It is said that the French King, Louis Philippe, once asked the

THE ALEXANDER COLUMN.

Emperor Nicholas for a similar column from his Finland quarries. The Tsar, however, begged to be excused. "I do not wish," he said, "to send you a smaller one, a similar one I cannot afford, and a larger one it is impossible to obtain."

As we turned away from this noble monolith, on the night of our arrival in St. Petersburg, the slowly descending globe of the northern sun was flooding the city with a marvelous radiance, and gilding brightly the summit of the column. In fact, so far into the night did this illumination linger, clothing the angel and his cross with glory, that we could almost fancy it unwilling to leave them, until they

THE PALACE QUAY.

should again be greeted by the kiss of dawn.

Close by the Alexander Column stands the Winter Palace, — one of the largest buildings in the world, — and, during the greater part of the year, the residence of the Tsar. It is imposingly designed, for its dimensions are gigantic. It is also superbly situated, for close beside it rolls the Neva, like a flood of silver.

MEMORIAL CHAPEL TO ALEXANDER.

How vast must be the expense of keeping this monstrous residence in perfect order! It would be great enough, if managed honestly; but it has recently come to light that there have been "political" housecleaners in this imperial abode. Thus, for a long time fifteen hundred roubles were charged annually merely for brooms to sweep this palace; but, on examination, it was found that, at that rate, fifty brooms must have been worn out every day during the reign of Alexander II. From this single item one can imagine what other frauds have been perpetrated here, and can under-stand the re-mark of the Tsar Nicho-las, when he exclaimed sadly, "My son and I are the only men in Russia who do not steal."

In winter, when a ball

THE HOME OF THE TSAR.

is given, these halls are sometimes converted into tropical gardens, by the introduction of exotic plants and flowers. The guests then pass, as if by magic, from snow-covered streets and a temperature of thirty degrees below zero, into the gorgeous splendor of a southern carnival; and, only a few feet distant from icicles and the glacial blasts of the north, they inhale the fragrance of orange blossoms, and feel upon their cheeks a warmth soft as the breath of Egypt. Such scenes are characteristic, too, of entertainments given by wealthy nobles; for, born amid snow and ice, the Russians have a passion for these emblems of a warmer clime.

In one room of the Winter Palace, guarded night and day, are kept the Crown Jewels of Russia. It would be difficult to imagine anything more magnificent than the imperial crown. It is in the form of a dome, the summit of which consists of a cross of large diamonds resting on an immense ruby. This ruby, with its cross, is poised upon arches of diamonds, whose bases

THE EMPRESS' ROOM.

A PALATIAL HALL.

rest upon a circle of twenty - eight other diamonds, that clasp the brow of the Emperor. The crown of the Empress, also, contains no less than one hundred splendid diamonds; and is, perhaps, the most beautiful mass of these precious stones ever formed into a single ornament.

The chief of the superb collection is the Orloff diamond, which sparkles on the summit of the imperial sceptre. Its history is as interesting as the stone itself is dazzling. It formed at one time the eye of an idol in a temple of

India. A French soldier, pre-
tending to have been con-
verted to the native re-
ligion, gained access
to the idol's temple
one dark night, and,
by some surgical op-
eration best known
to himself, deprived
the deity of its bright
eye, and fled with the
prize. Then, after pass-
ing through several hands,
it was finally purchased, for
over half a million of dollars,

SUMMER IN THE WINTER PALACE.

by the famous Count Orloff, who laid it at the feet of Catharine II., as the most magnificent jewel in the world.

One portrait in the Winter Palace made an indelible
impression on my mind. It was that of Alexander II. It

THE BALL-ROOM.

showed few traces of
his youthful beauty
and magnificent
physique; for the last
years of his reign
changed him greatly.
The settled melan-
choly, characteristic
of the Romanoffs, ap-
parently reached in
him its climax. His
eyes, said to have
been always sad, as-
sumed at last a
pathetic expression,

as though the spectres of conspiracy, assassination, Nihilism, disappointment, and thwarted ambition were preying, vulture-like, upon his heart. In look-ing at them I could half believe that they foresaw the awful doom which Destiny was holding for him, — waiting until the fatal hour should come. That hour came all too soon, and proved more tragic than even in his wildest dream he could have imagined.

ALEXANDER II.

It was on the 21st of March, 1881, that the remains of Alexander II., killed by the bombs of Nihilists, were conveyed with solemn pag-eantry from the Winter Palace to the last resting-place of the Romanoffs, on the opposite bank of the Neva. So long was the mournful procession that it took two hours to pass a given point. It was of almost unexampled splendor, for all that was regal and warlike in the empire had its representation there. The funeral car was of ebony and silver, and was drawn by

THE WINTER PALACE.

eight black horses, shrouded in sable draperies; while the
coffin of the Tsar was nearly hidden by a golden pall, lined
with white satin. Sixteen generals held the silken cords of the
canopy above;
and behind his
murdered father
walked Alexan-
der III., in his
imperial solitude,
bearing alone his
griefs and his re-
sponsibilities.

If possible,
more solemn still
must have been
the sight of the
silent thousands
who lined the

THE NEVA AND WINTER
PALACE.

A VILLA ON THE NEVA.

shores of the
Neva, until the
river seemed to
flow between two
banks of pale and
saddened faces.
Bareheaded and
mute they stood
there for hours,
many of them
praying for the
soul of the dead Tsar; while hundreds of priests, clad in their
ecclesiastical robes, and bearing tapers in their hands, were
chanting on the air a solemn requiem.

If the Tsar stands at any window, in the portion of his palace fronting the river, he can perceive on the opposite bank the Bastille of Russia, — the Fortress of Petropaulovski. Probably no prison now standing in the world has witnessed more cruelty and suffering than this. Walls, it is said, have ears; but, had they tongues, what horrible deeds could be disclosed by these dark, icy dungeons, situ-

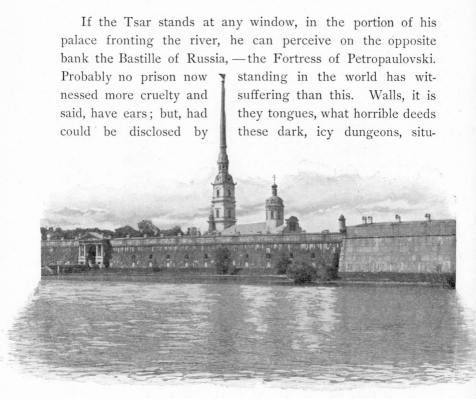

THE FORTRESS OF SS. PETER AND PAUL.

ated below the level of the Neva — the walls and floors slimy with dampness! Here Alexis, the rebellious son of Peter the Great, died, after protracted torture; and here a number of political prisoners were drowned during an overflow of the Neva.

A curious ceremony takes place in front of the Winter Palace, in the spring, when the ice breaks up in the Neva. Naturally, this is a period of great rejoicing, and the first boat that crosses the liberated stream conveys the governor of the fortress to the palace, where he presents a glass of Neva water to the Tsar. The Emperor drinks it, and

returns the goblet to the governor, filled to the brim with
gold coin. Such, at least, was the custom till Alexander
III. noticed that every year the glass increased in size,
requiring more gold pieces to fill it. Accordingly, he named
a certain sum that should be placed in the goblet, irrespec-
tive of its capacity, and which he deemed sufficient to reward,
if not to satisfy, the Ganymede of the Neva.

Standing on the bank of a canal, and connected with
the Winter Palace by a bridge, — the form of which reminds
us of the Venetian Bridge of Sighs, — is another prominent
building, the Hermitage. Catharine II. caused this to be
built, much as Frederick the Great erected, near Berlin,
his pretty villa, Sans Souci, as a refuge from the cares
of State; and here she passed many of her even-
ings, surrounded by French philosophers, musicians, and
artists, all of whom were obliged, according to the laws

LUMBER BOATS ON THE NEVA.

of the Hermitage, to
leave behind them,
at the threshold, every consideration of precedence, rank,
and birth, and to meet on terms of absolute equality. Thus,
on the walls of this palace was a notice forbidding guests to
rise when the Empress came into the room, to speak un-

kindly to any one present, or of any one absent, or even to
look ill-tempered! They were also reminded to leave their

THE HERMITAGE.

quarrels at the door,
with their swords
and hats. Small fines
were inflicted for the
violation of these
rules, and the money
was given to the
poor. So thoroughly
unconventional was
life in the Hermi-
tage that the Em-
press, when playing
games, paid her for-
feits like the other
guests. On one oc-
casion, for example,

she was told to sit down on the floor, and she obeyed at once.

PORTICO OF THE HERMITAGE.

THE ADMIRALTY QUAY.

Catharine II. was certainly an extraordinary woman; intellectually great enough, to be called by the French philosopher, Didérot, "The candlestick bearing the light of the age"; sufficiently voluptuous, to be still passionately in love at sixty-seven, and to be styled "the Semiramis of the North"; yet brave enough, to risk her life and beauty by being almost the first in her empire to be inoculated for small-pox; every inch an empress, yet treating others with a simplicity which put them immediately at their ease, and able to rule her empire well, though lovable and popular with all. "To tell the truth," she said, "I have never

THE MONUMENT TO CATHARINE II.

fancied myself extremely beautiful; but I have the art of pleasing which, I think, is my greatest gift."

The Hermitage is no longer a royal residence. Like the Louvre at Paris, it has now become the principal art museum of the capital. I was surprised to see the treasures which this comparatively youthful nation has secured. The truth is, that for many years the Russian Government has spent

A HALL IN THE HERMITAGE.

large sums of money in this direction, and, it is said, has had agents ready to outbid the world for any master-piece that might be offered for sale.

Here, cer-tainly, is the best collection of Spanish pictures to be found out-side of Spain ; one room, alone, containing no less than thirty genuine Murillos, some of which seemed to me as fine as any I had seen in Madrid and Seville. Moreover, in no other art museum in the world are there such ornaments as in this Hermi-tage. The walls are either ele-gantly frescoed, or covered with silken tapestry. Sofas and chairs of the same rich material invite the weary tourist to repose ; while the magnificent vases of por-phyry, stands of Siberian marble,

THE STAIRCASE IN THE HERMITAGE.

tables of malachite, candelabra of violet jasper, and urns of lapis-lazuli, which decorate these halls, are of incalculable value, and would, of themselves, almost repay a special visit to Russia.

Most of the lovely statues in the Hermitage are works of modern sculptors, but are, probably, none the less attractive on that account to the majority of travelers. As I beheld these charming figures, I could not doubt the statement that Alexander II., who personally selected many of them, had excellent judgment in affairs of art. It would be easy for a hermit to renounce the world, if he could make this Hermitage his cell; for here are the marvels of the globe, glowing upon canvas, crystallized in marble, carved in ivory, woven in tapestry, and offering

THE WOUNDED NYMPH.

delightful illustrations of the world's beauty and progress.

In one of the finest squares of St. Petersburg is an equestrian statue of the Tsar Nicholas. He may be called an ideal Russian autocrat, a civilized Peter the Great. His very person was majestic. More than six feet in height and finely proportioned, his appearance was commanding.

The impression which he produced on his people was extraordinary. His courage was put to the test on the very ~y of his coronation. A revolt had taken place among the . The fate of his dynasty hung in the balance. With-

out a moment's hesitation Nicholas embraced his wife, to
whom he was devotedly attached, and said to her, "Farewell, in half an hour I shall be absolute master of those
mutineers, or else a corpse." He then descended to the
square, where the rebellious regiments were assembled.
Rising in his stirrups, with flashing eyes and imperious
voice and gesture, as if he were the representative of Jove

THE STATUE OF NICHOLAS I.

himself, he cried, "Return to your ranks!" The men obeyed.
"Down on your knees and beg for mercy!" The soldiers
dropped upon their knees. This seems, perhaps, incredible,
yet there are men like Cæsar, Napoleon, and Nicholas who
were born to command their fellow-men, and are instinctively
obeyed. On that occasion, for example, a conspirator, who
had sworn to assassinate Nicholas, approached four times to
do it, and every time his arm dropped powerless to his side.

UNIVERSITY QUAY.

One of the most imposing structures in St. Petersburg is the Admiralty, the centre of the Naval Department of Russia. The front of this gigantic building is half a mile in length, and from its finely decorated tower rises a slender shaft of gold, which is one of the first objects visible on approaching the city, and may be likened to a glittering exclamation point of wonder at Peter's great achievements. Although he found his empire without a fishing-boat, Peter, nevertheless, bequeathed to it a victorious navy, and gave it commercial relations with almost

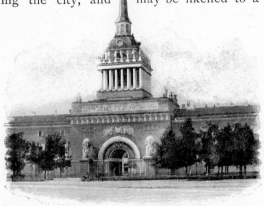

THE TOWER OF THE ADMIRALTY.

every other nation on the globe; and this, notwithstanding the fact that the harbor of his capital is for six months in the year almost as inaccessible to ships as the North Pole.

Filled with such thoughts, I stood with admiration and respect before the statue of the man who could conceive and execute such stupendous plans. He is portrayed reining in his steed at full gallop, on the very verge of a precipice. His face looks toward the Neva, and his outstretched hand seems beckoning to the world to gaze upon the vast metropolis which, compelled by a will that knew no obstacle, appears to have risen to, and to be resting upon, the surface of the river, like a fair lily with resplendent colors. Even the pedestal of this monument is remarkable. It is a mighty mass of granite, weighing fifteen hundred tons, and was brought hither with immense labor from Finland. No other stone, however, would the Russians have; for it was on this rock that Peter stood and watched the victory of his infant navy over his enemies, the Swedes.

It is only right and just that St. Petersburg should bear the name of its founder, since it is impossible to take a step here without being reminded of him. Do we walk on pavements? It is due to his engineering that we are not sinking in a swamp. Do we observe the city's animated life? It is the life breathed into it by its creator. Do we admire its imposing palaces, granite monoliths, its churches built of marble, bronze, and gold, its endless avenues where hundreds can march abreast? It was at his command that they were reared, and on a soil, too, into which whole forests had at first to disappear; so that the foundations of this city sink almost as far  below the surface of the ground as its resplendent spires rise toward Heaven. Truly, in view of the stupendous difficulties of creating this great city of the North, its faults (due largely to its youth and rapid growth) disappear beside the marvelous fact that it exists at all.

PETER THE GREAT.

Nothing was to me more interesting, in the Russian capital, than the little house which Peter was content to occupy, while urging on in person the mighty work of building. This home of Peter, erected largely by his own hands,

KAZAN CATHEDRAL.

is kept within an outer structure, like a jewel in a box. It is composed of logs and consists of only three apartments, — a bedroom, dining-room, and kitchen. But what a contrast between the rooms of Peter then and now! His bedroom,

THE HOUSE AND CHURCH OF PETER THE GREAT.

for example, has been changed into a gorgeous chapel, with marble floor and alabaster ceiling, and walls gleaming with paintings and magnificent gems; for Peter (much to his astonishment, no doubt, if he is aware of it) has become a saint, and the vast empire, which he so greatly influenced and modernized, now glorifies him in forty different languages; since from the Polar Sea to the Caspian, and from the Gulf of Finland to the Chinese Wall, the name of Peter is spoken almost as of some deity.

From the day when his political enemies tried to murder Peter in childhood, and he was rescued by his mother, who fled with him to a sacred shrine, and, pointing to the picture

PETER SAVED BY HIS MOTHER.

of the Virgin and her Child, forbade the assassins to advance, his whole life reads like a romance. To realize fully what he accomplished when he came to manhood, we must remember that his entire empire was then inland. It is true the billows of the Polar Sea broke on the icebergs of his northern coast, but that shore was practically worthless. Of other oceans he had none. Between his western boundary and the Baltic stood the Swedes; between his southern limit and the Black Sea were the Turks; and even the sunny lands, bordering on the Caspian, were held by the effeminate Persians. All the great natural gateways of his realm, therefore, were not only locked, but the keys were in the possession of his enemies.

Yet, when one looks on some of the mighty rivers in the Russian Empire, such as the Volga, the Neva, and the Dnieper, he realizes how those noble streams, sweeping to their different oceans, must have lured the young Tsar's fancy down their channels, and kindled in his breast the great ambition of his life, — to open Russia to the sea. "It is not land that I need," he cried repeatedly, "but water." To burst the barriers that encompassed him, and secure an exit to the outer world, he perceived was the sole means of lifting his empire from the slough of barbarism, and changing it from a dull, Asiatic

NATIVE WASHERWOMEN.

monarchy into an active European state. Now, to detect this
at the start, and then to form a plan to which he adhered all
his life, in spite of unexampled obstacles, proves Peter to have
been a man of genius. The world has seldom seen such a
display of courage and determination as that which Peter gave
when, setting at defiance the opposition of his nobles and the

THE VOLGA.

prejudices of his people, he deliberately left his throne for a
time and went to Europe; not to enjoy a royal holiday, but
rather to exchange his sceptre for an ax, and to acquire a
thorough knowledge of those maritime affairs on which his
heart was set. Since he had resolved to have a fleet, he must
learn how to build it, and then must secure a sea on which his
ships could sail. He had already sent fifty Russian nobles
to study civilized life in Italy and Germany. But this was

THE GUARD-ROOM.

not enough. To set them an example, he must himself do what he had ordered them to accomplish.

Peter naturally chose Holland as the school which he would attend; for that country was then the centre of the maritime world. During his stay there, while making his investigations, he fairly exhausted all his guides by his insatiable curiosity. Of course, his first attention was given to the art of ship-building; but he also visited manufactories and rope-walks; watched surgical operations in the hospitals, and acquired the art of blood-letting and tapping for the dropsy. Moreover, the young Tsar was so charmed by the manipulations of a dentist that he called him to his lodgings, learned how

WHERE PETER WENT TO SCHOOL.

to use his implements of torture, and thenceforth amused himself, in his leisure moments, by practicing on his wretched followers.

Although Peter worked so indefatigably, he showed himself at times to be little more than an uncouth savage, to whom the laws and customs of society were unbearable. Artificial articles of toilet, for example, were quite new to him. On one occasion, he snatched a new and stylish wig from the head of the master of ceremonies at the Dutch Court, and, after looking at it for a moment with supreme disgust, threw it upon the floor. When he danced with the Holland ladies, he could not understand the stiffness of their corsets, and exclaimed, "The bones of these Dutch women seem to me devilish hard."

PETER IN HOLLAND.

"Who are those men?" he asked, when in London, pointing to some English barristers wearing their wigs and gowns. "Lawyers," was the reply "Lawyers!" repeated Peter, "what is the use of so many? I have only two in my whole empire, and I mean to hang one of them as soon as I return." Yet, notwithstanding his ferocity and coarseness, Peter must be regarded as one of the world's great men. The difficulties which he met were almost insurmountable; for the entire nation was against him, — still he executed his reforms with a tenacity of will almost sublime.

A Russian writer represents him standing alone and pulling upward, while millions of opponents pulled the other way.
The Russians, more than any other people in Europe, have
been opposed to change.   For generations they had looked
upon foreigners with contempt.   "Novelty brings calamity,"
is one of their proverbs.   Whenever I think of Peter I am
reminded of the painting that represents a Russian driver
struggling heroically in a storm that threatens to destroy

OVERCOMING OBSTACLES.

him. It was just
such a spirit
which animated
Peter. Nothing
discouraged
him. Thus, in
his early con-
flicts with the
Swedes for the
possession of
the Baltic, he
was repeatedly
defeated; but he
was not disheart-
ened. After sev-
eral years of
such misfortunes he wrote to his wife: "I expected to be
defeated at the start; but finally the Swedes will teach me
how to beat them."   That sentence indicates his character.
What can eventually overcome a man who never knows
when he is beaten, and after every fall rises, Antæus-like,
to grimly try again, at any sacrifice of men and money?
"Glory to God!" he wrote, some twelve months later, "I
have gotten my Russian soldiers now so that they will beat
the Swedes when we are four to their one; by and by they
will do it on equal terms."   In truth they did so, enabling

A HEAVY LOAD.

Peter to secure the coveted situation by the ocean, where he located and built St. Petersburg.

We may, however, be very sure that, when shut out from the observation of the world, Peter often suffered bitterly from rage and shame. Once, for example, the Swedes defeated him and took so many Russians prisoners, that

A RUSSIAN CAB.

Charles XII. could not keep them. Charles, therefore, took away their weapons and set them free, saying: "Go home and raise cabbages; that is all you are good for. You are not soldiers!" At the same time, in jest, he caused the long gowns of the Russian prisoners to be cut off at the hips, so that the only way the wretched men could keep the lower part of their bodies covered was by holding up their skirts with both hands. The Swedish army roared with laughter to see the Russians in this plight. A medal, also, was struck off in Stockholm, to commemorate the event. On one side, the Russians were portrayed as running away and holding up their robes; and on the other was a picture of Peter, with these words, "And Peter went out and wept bitterly."

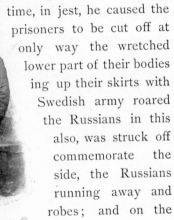

A RUSSIAN PEASANT.

This experience prompted the Tsar to institute a practical reform. In those days the Russian peasants wore much longer gowns than they do now. On his return from western Europe, therefore, these trailing garments struck Peter as absurd; for, though they served as a protection against cold, they were extremely inconvenient for laborers and soldiers. Accordingly, he ordered them to be shortened. Still worse, however, in Peter's eyes were the long, unkempt Russian beards. These he resolved should disappear entirely. He would not have a person near him who did not shave, and levied on every beard worn by the upper classes an annual tax of from sixty to two hundred dollars. To realize what this meant, we should bear in mind that this was as great an innovation as if the Chinese Emperor should order all his subjects to cut off their queues. Moreover, the Russian priests declared that to remove the beard was to deface the image of God. Most of the people, therefore, paid the tax in order to keep their beards. But Peter was inexorable, and placed at every gate a score or two of barbers and tailors whose duty it was, under the eyes of soldiery, to seize when passing each man who had not obeyed the order, and, by the aid of shears and razors, rob him of petticoat and beard at one fell swoop.

A STREET SHRINE.

A still more radical and important change effected by Peter had reference to the female sex. Up to his time Russian women had been secluded in a kind of harem; or if they ventured into the streets, they were forced to put on veils, or ride in carriages with curtains drawn. Wife-beating was a universal custom. The priests merely advised men not to use too thick a club. A Russian proverb makes a husband say to his wife, "I love thee like my soul, but I dust thee like my

A PALACE GUARD IN ST. PETERSBURG.

jacket." A historian mentions a Muscovite woman who, having married a foreigner, did not believe herself loved because
he did not beat her. What a picture the Russia of one hundred years ago presents, compared to the witty, social intercourse of France or of England! In those times, also, a Russian husband saw his bride unveiled for the first time at the
wedding banquet. But Peter roughly changed all this, and
decreed that six weeks before every marriage a betrothal
should take
place, and that
thenceforth the
bridal pair might
see each other
freely; and, if
they were not
satisfied, might
break the en-
gagement.

   Shocking as
this appeared to
his people, worse
still was to come;
for Peter further
horrified his no-

AN IMPERIAL BOUDOIR.

bles by ordering them to bring their wives and daughters into
society. He made a law that social gatherings should be held
three times a week, in the houses of the nobility in turn,
besides an occasional ball in his own palace. At these assem-
blies men and women were ordered to appear dressed in the
European style, and even to dance together; while, most
curious of all, French and Swedish prisoners of war were
admitted to these gatherings, to serve as models in society
manners. One marvels that his subjects did not rise a hundred times to depose or murder Peter; but he maintained his

absolute authority, and even in his rules of social etiquette, governed his subjects with a rod of iron. Once, when his Prime Minister, Prince Menchikoff, forgot himself, and danced with his sword on, Peter gave him a blow that made the blood flow freely. At another time, when an unlucky officer forgot to salute his partner after dancing, he knocked him down.

PETER THE GREAT.

Yet, after all, it is sad to realize that this great toiler for his country's civilization never really understood what civilization meant. He left no code of laws founded on noble principles of justice. Material progress alone kindled his enthusiasm. He did not try to elevate the morals of his people, and the result was well expressed in the rough words of Didérot, who said, "The Russians, as fashioned by Peter, were rotten before they were ripe!"

It is an illustration of Peter's peculiar character, that his life alternated between great physical exertion and wild dissipation. Shortly before his

THE BANQUET-HALL.

death, he gave a banquet at which three thousand bottles of wine were emptied, and Peter took so prominent a part in their depletion, that he kept to his bed for a week. Nevertheless, as soon as he was able to go out, he went to his new foundry, and, with his own hands, hammered out a sheet of iron weighing a hundred pounds.

In the ballroom of the palace, which he built at Peterhof, hangs a painting that represents an actual event in Peter's life: when, in a fearful

IN THE TSAR'S PALACE.

storm on Lake Ladoga, he pushed aside the trembling sailors and brought the boat in safety to the shore. Physically, Peter was a giant; so tall, that we stand like pygmies by the rod which indicates his height; so strong, that his walk-ing-stick, still kept in the museum, was a bar of iron; so

THE PAINTING OF PETER.

skillful, that he made with his own hands his house, his furni-ture, and boats. The character of the man was, in some ways, won-derfully great; in others, pitiful-ly small. He was a strange crea-tion, half colos-sus and half dwarf. Of this he was himself aware. "I wish to reform my empire," he once said, sadly, "but I cannot reform myself."

Yet Peter was a man of noble impulses. Soon after his recovery from the illness caused by his carousal, he beheld a vessel full of soldiers and sailors helplessly drifting at the mercy of the winds and waves, and driven toward the shore. With his accustomed heroism, he hurried to their rescue. All night long he stood in the icy water to his waist, and with his own hands saved the lives of twenty men. But this exposure brought on an inflammation, which rapidly developed dangerous symptoms. Peter does not appear to have been well treated, for a celebrated Dutch physician, on learning the facts in the case, exclaimed, "Merciful Heavens!

UP THE NEVA, FROM PALACE BRIDGE.

Was it possible to allow that great man to die, when he might have been cured by a pennyworth of medicine?" Still, in those hours when pain appeared his sole connecting link with earth, he characteristically strove to give another world to Russia; for it was then that the navigator Bering received from Peter's hand those orders, which were to extend his empire across the body of water known as Bering's Strait, from Siberia into Alaska.

Although the Tsar fought against his anguish like a dying Hercules, the pain became at last so intense as to wring from him frightful shrieks and groans. Finally, unable to articulate, he motioned for a slate on which to write his will. It was a thrilling moment! The fate of mil-

lions hung upon his signature. He seized the pencil and scrawled three words only, "Give all to," — then his hand dropped upon the bed.

Cruel caprice of destiny! The autocrat whose slightest wish was a command, the man whose prominent character-istic had been his

THE TSAR'S BEDROOM.

unexampled power of volition, had died without a will.

Fifteen miles from St. Petersburg, and easily reached by the first railroad ever built in Russia, is Tsars-Koe-Selo, one of the summer homes of the imperial family. Catharine II. loved this place especially, and spent enormous sums upon its embellishment. Its lovely park is eighteen miles in circumference. Upon its pretty lake were formerly several swans, of which the youthful daughter of the Tsar Nicholas was very fond. This child died at an early age, and, ever since, the white swans which she loved have been replaced by black swans, as though they were in mourning for their young mistress. In a pavilion adjoining the lake is hung the portrait of this little Princess, and beneath

THE LAKE.

TSARS-KOE-SELO.

it is one of her childish sayings, which startles us when we think it referred to the despotic ruler, Nicholas. It is this, "I know, Papa, that you have no greater pleasure than that of making Mamma happy."

Beyond the lake, a pretty river winds through the park in graceful curves, with numerous bridges of fantastic and beautiful designs. This garden of Tsars-Koe-Selo is one of the most beautifully kept enclosures in the world. On account of the severity of the Russian climate, its trees and

IN THE PARK.

flowers have to be watched and cultivated with the utmost tenderness. Catharine II. used to say, "In Russia we have not summer and winter, but only a white winter and a green winter." An invalid soldier here commands an army of five hundred gardeners. After each falling leaf a veteran runs, and every spear of grass is carefully drawn from lake and river. The cost of this lavish care amounts, it is said, to fifty thousand dollars a year; but the result is a park that is kept in the order of a ball-room.

Entering the palace, we found a display of the same extravagance that formerly characterized its outer walls. One beautiful apartment is called the "Chinese" room, because much of its furniture and

THE RIVER.

decorations are modeled after the styles of the Celestial Empire. Another is the hall of "Lapis-Lazuli," the sides of which are beautifully inlaid with that rare stone; while the floor is of ebony, adorned with mosaic flowers made of mother-of-pearl. Still another is called the "Amber" room, because its walls are literally covered with that precious substance. Even the chairs in this apartment are made of amber, and amber chessmen stand on an amber board.

THE CHINESE ROOM.

In striking contrast, however, to this splendor, the private apartments of the Russian sovereigns are extremely plain. I was especially impressed with the austerity of the bedroom of the Emperor Nicholas, where he died of a broken heart, because of the disastrous results of the. Crimean War. The room remains as when he occupied it. Probably no reader of these pages has one so plain; for the floor is carpetless, and the bed is a narrow frame of iron. On the walls are a few simple pictures of Sevastopol, and on the floor is a pair of slippers that he wore for years, and which, it is plain to see, were often mended.

What was true of Nicholas, was true also of his son. The study of the Emperor Alexander II. is very simply decorated. The furniture is upholstered in leather, and only a few portraits of his children, relatives, and soldiers adorn the walls. Whether the old domestic, who showed us through the palace, suspected that we had dynamite about our persons, I know not; but he seemed quite reluctant to admit us to these private rooms.

THE BEDROOM OF NICHOLAS.

Accordingly, our guide informed him in a whisper that we were really Russians of high rank, who, since we were traveling *incognito*, chose to speak a foreign language.

THE STUDY OF ALEXANDER II.

I was not responsible for this lie; but either that, or a rouble slipped into his hand, produced the desired effect, and we were admitted.

In our subsequent tour of the palace, I was in constant dread lest that servant should ask us for

our Russian titles.   In that event we should have had to resort
to the device of three Americans who, on their travels here,
had taken Russian names.   These proved so difficult to remember and pronounce, that finally they invented some far
easier to recall, since they were based on their respective looks
or occupations.   Thus, one who practiced dentistry, called
himself "Count Pull-a-Tusky"; the second, who was a dis-
tiller, took the title of "Prince Cask-O'-Whisky"; while the
third, who had the misfortune to be bald, was styled by his
companions, "General Hair-all-off."

A good story is told of the Tsar Alexander I.   One
morning, entering with his wife the elegantly furnished bou-

doir of the Em-
press, they found,
on the table, a
small p a c k a g e
awaiting   them.
That was before
the days of Nihil-
ism and of dyna-
mite — hence the
Emperor opened
it without hesita-
tion.   It proved
to be a volume
of poems written
by a man who,
although talented
and witty, was

THE RECEPTION HALL OF THE EMPRESS.

poverty-stricken, as indeed most poets have always been.   The
Emperor read the book, and was so well pleased with its
contents, that he caused a hundred bank-notes, of one hundred roubles each, to be bound in a book, and wrote on its
title-page the words, "Poems of the Emperor Alexander."

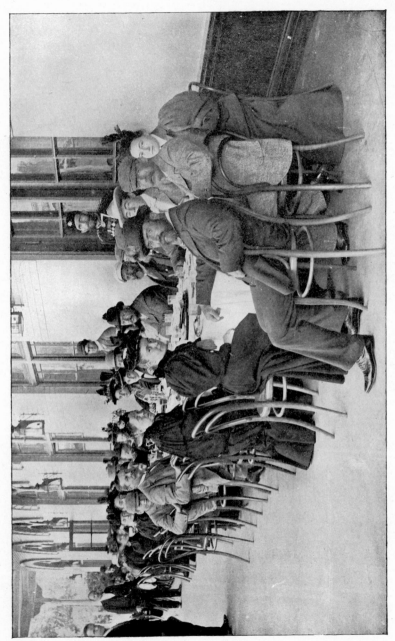

GROUP AT RAILROAD STATION.

This he sent to the needy poet. Soon after this act of imperial generosity, a ball was given here. Among the guests
was the delighted poet, who hastened to the Tsar to express
his thanks. "Well," said Alexander, "how do you like my

poems?" "Very
much, indeed,
Sire," was the re-
ply, "as far as I
have read them;
but I have as yet
seen only the first
volume." The
Tsar smiled, and
the next day or-
dered another
similar book of
bank-notes to be
made, entitled,
"Poems of the
Emperor Alex-
ander: Volume

A HALL IN TSARS-KOE-SELO.

Second." This time, however, on the last page the Emperor
had written with his own hand, "The End."

Rivaling Tsars-Koe-Selo in interest, is Peterhof, — another
summer residence of the imperial family, also in the vicinity
of St. Petersburg. No sooner had we entered its extensive
park than we found ourselves in the midst of a multitude
of fountains, which in number, design, and beauty are unsurpassed, even by those of Versailles. Peterhof is another
result of the indomitable energy of Peter the Great. If
Louis XIV., he said, had created fountains on a sandy plain
near Paris, why should not he do as much along the marshes
of the Neva? With Peter no delay was possible. Within
two months after the autocrat's order had been given, the

thousands of workmen, whom he had summoned to the pro-
digious task, announced that the canals and aqueducts were
ready.   Another army of laborers was equally expeditious
in the construction of the palace, avenues, and villas.
Statues and ornaments, also, sprang up as if by magic;
and since trees were already abundant, the entire park and
buildings of Peterhof were constructed within a year.   In

THE PALACE OF PETERHOF.

his impatience, Peter is said to have felled many
trees himself, swinging the ax with a force that none of
his workmen could equal.

One room in the palace of Peterhof is unique; for its
walls are entirely paneled with female portraits, painted for
Catharine II. by a favorite artist.   It is rather bewildering to stand environed at one time by eight hundred and
sixty-three pictures of beautiful young women.   Yet there is
no monotony in them.   Each face as well as each attitude is
different.   One pretty girl is knitting busily; another peeps
archly from behind a curtain; a third weeps; while still

another buries herself to her ears in fur, leaving visible only a pair of rosy lips and dreamy eyes.

The fountains form the most remarkable feature of Peterhof. There seems to be no limit to their number and variety. One, for example, is called the "Mountain of Gold," because the water flows over a flight

THE ROOM OF PORTRAITS.

of gilded steps, which give it, when illuminated, the appearance of a cataract of molten gold. Nymphs, lions, rivergods, and heroes of mythology and history all figure in them, until the perspective is bewildering; while, not content with these, the architect designed long rows of single fountains, and pyramids of water, and even artificial trees, each leaf of which sends forth a silvery stream. The most astonishing, however, represents Samson contending with a lion, from whose mouth a stream leaps forth to the height of eighty feet. Finally, the enormous flood of water from these various sources unites in one great volume, and rolls away like a wild mountain torrent toward the sea.

THE HALL OF BUSTS.

A fancy of the Tsar Nicholas was to make his pages and
servants, at the beat of a drum, charge on these fountains,
and, rushing furiously into their blinding streams, attempt to
capture them like batteries, and turn off the water with their
own hands. We may be tolerably sure, however, that Nicholas
himself never led the charge.

THE FOUNTAINS OF PETERHOF.

MOSCOW

MOSCOW

OSCOW is further east than Jerusalem. Like Constantinople, it is situated where the two great divisions of our globe, the Orient and the Occident, forever gaze into each other's eyes. Beyond this city are half-civilized lands and races, extending in barbaric wildness to Tartary and China, or over the enormous area of Siberia toward Alaska, our own frost - covered storm-door of the North. But as a mighty continent rises slowly from the sea, so from the barbarism of those eastern lands the Russian Empire is gradually emerging; and Moscow is its lofty

MOSCOW.

headland — its frontier city, faced Janus-like to east and west — a golden link between the Russia which has been and that which is to be.

I do not wonder that the soldiers of Napoleon's army, after their weary march of nearly two thousand miles, cheered with a frenzy of enthusiasm as the enchanting vista of this city burst upon their view. No foreigner can look upon it without deep emotion; and as for the Russian peasants, whenever they approach this sacred city of the empire, and see its gilded turrets gleam like golden helmets in the sun, they often fall upon their knees and weep for joy, moved to an ecstasy of religious feeling, like that which thrilled the hosts of the crusaders when they first gazed upon Jerusalem.

Five minutes after we had left the railway station, however, we needed no argument to convince us that Moscow, like most Oriental cities, has a decidedly "seamy side." So fearfully and wonderfully constructed are some of its pave-

THE KREMLIN FROM ACROSS THE RIVER.

ments that, in our transit from the station to the hotel, we
were chiefly occupied in holding on, for dear life, to the
sides of an antediluvian droshky, the motion of which sug-
gested the sensation of riding upon the back of a runaway
camel, as we bounded along on a chaotic mass of muddy
earth, into which sharp stones appeared   to have been oc-

A MOSCOW STREET OMNIBUS.

casionally dropped, like raisins in a pudding.   Whenever the
droshky struck one of those "raisins," I thought of home
and heaven simultaneously, and saw stars in a clear sky.

Moscow is one of the most irregularly built cities in the
world.   It is characteristic of a nation in a transition state.
Every building stands in striking contrast with its neigh-
bor. Thus, before a finely proportioned church, with lofty
towers and brilliant domes, is located the hut of a black-
smith; and at its side extends a row of cheap yellow cot-
tages. Miserable hovels, which we should expect to find in
the outskirts of a town, stand forth in Moscow beside a
palace or a cathedral, just as a Russian peasant — clad in
his sheepskin coat, wherein are concentrated the unsavory
odors of several generations — will remain, unconscious of
his filthiness, beside a man who is cleanly dressed.

Moreover, in Russian society there are said
to be contrasts no less striking than those
discoverable in Russian architecture. In reality, there are but two great social divisions
in Russia, — the cultivated class, of less than
a million, and the "Black Brood," numbering
about ninety millions. Between these there
is, however, an intermediate type, which
properly belongs to the uncultivated class.
It is that of the prosperous merchants, —
the *nouveaux riches*, who are anxious to
assume the airs and luxuries of the nobles,
and of whom the most ludicrous stories are

ONE OF THE BLACK BROOD.

told. An English traveler says that one of these suddenly
enriched traders evinced great pride in showing him over his
house, which was, indeed, furnished in sumptuous style.
Finally, in his sleeping-room, he called his attention to a
magnificent gilded bed. "What do you think of *that?*" he
asked, rubbing his hands exultantly. The traveler replied
that it was superb. "Is it not
so? Is it not so?" exclaimed
the Russian, smacking his
lips, and pointing out
the blue silk curtains
and white lace. "But
it cost me so much
that I don't sleep *on*
this bed, but *under*
it!"

One of the first
things to attract my
notice in Moscow was
the enormous number
of churches it contains.

BULBOUS DOMES.

PANORAMA FROM THE TOWER OF IVAN THE TERRIBLE.

Their architecture is peculiar. How singular are their bulbous domes! To use a homely but apt comparison, they call
to mind inverted onions. Still, they are not displeasing to
the eye. On the contrary, as they are usually gilded, these
are among the most attractive architectural ornaments in the
world. Moreover, the domes of Russian churches are surmounted by gilded crosses adorned with thin gilt chains.
On many of them a crescent is seen beneath the cross; this
elevation of the emblem of Christianity above that of Moham-
medanism being intended as a
symbol of the triumph of
the Russians over their
Tartar adversaries. The
exterior walls of these
churches are, also,
frequently covered
with frescos or
painted green or
dark red, occasionally
even in brighter colors.
Thus, one of the con-
vents near Moscow has dove-
colored walls and silver domes.
It is pleasant to remember that

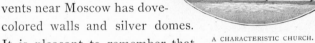

A CHARACTERISTIC CHURCH.

beneath these domes there are no favored places, obtainable
by money or birth. Even in Russia, noble and peasant
kneel, side by side, on terms of absolute equality to offer up
their prayers to God.

Of all the sanctuaries in Moscow the most magnificent is the
famous Church of the Saviour, whose splendor rivals that of
any other temple in the world. It was begun, in 1813, to commemorate the expulsion of the French from Russia, and is a
most imposing structure. It is visible from every quarter of
the city, and combines majesty of proportion with elegance of

decoration. The stone, of which it is composed, is of a delicate cream color, standing forth in beautiful relief against the
azure of the sky. Its form is, of course, that of the Greek
cross, and its magnificent dome gleams like a miniature sun
surrounded by four radiant satellites. Around the walls extends
a frieze of life-sized figures. Yet, beautiful as it thus appears,
its exterior gives only a faint hint of the treasures that it
contains. Its pavement is of va- riegated marble, and its
walls are covered with beautiful expanses of Siberian
jasper, porphyry, malachite, and alabaster, all exquisitely polished and cut in a variety of forms.
Moreover, here and there, these splendid

THE CHURCH OF THE SAVIOUR.

ornaments are interspersed with life-sized or co-lossal pictures in mosaic, frequent-ly encrusted with jewels; while the mighty dome it-self is filled with a wonderful and awe - inspiring painting repre-senting the Trinity.

SEEN FROM A DISTANCE.

I dare not hazard an estimate of the entire cost of this church, and I have found none that I could accept with confidence; but I may say, to illustrate the richness of its ornamentation, that one comparatively small section of Siberian jasper, inserted like a medallion in a marble wall, cost no less than fifteen thousand dollars.

Moreover, it should be remembered that this is the second great cathedral which Russia has built during the last seventy years; St. Isaac's in St. Petersburg having been begun in 1819, and completed in 1858, after an expenditure of about twenty million dollars. A third cathedral, nearly as large, is also in process of construction at Nijni Novgorod. The Church of the Saviour is particularly beautiful when its gilded domes are glittering in the long, fascinating northern twilight which makes the Russian summer so attractive.

> "Oh the splendor of the city
> When the sun is in the west!
> Ruddy gold on spire and belfry,
> Gold on Moskwa's placid breast;

Till the twilight, soft and sombre,
    Falls on wall and street and square,
And the domes and towers in shadow
    Stand like silent monks at prayer."

There is an institution in Moscow which no traveler should fail to visit. It is the Foundling Hospital, into which about thirteen thousand infants are admitted annually. It is said that no cities in the world surpass those of Russia in the comforts provided for outcast children. The Government grants, yearly, a million dollars to this hospital alone; yet there is another nearly as large as this in St. Petersburg. In many cities of Europe, when a child is brought to such an asylum, a bell is rung and the door turns upon a pivot so as to present to the applicant a little table. Upon this the infant is laid. The door then continues its revolution, and the child is wheeled gently within the walls of the hospital never again, perhaps, to be seen by its parents. In this institution, however, there

THE FOUNDLING HOSPITAL.

CHURCH OF THE MONASTERY.

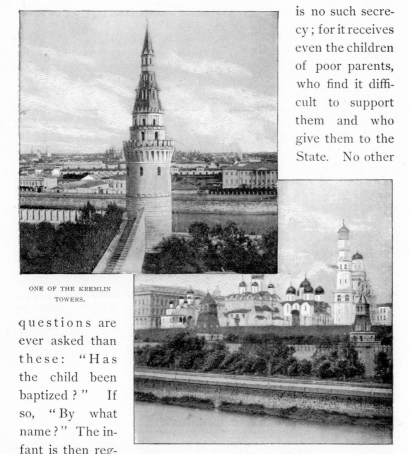

is no such secre-
cy; for it receives
even the children
of poor parents,
who find it diffi-
cult to support
them and who
give them to the
State.   No other

ONE OF THE KREMLIN
TOWERS.

questions are
ever asked than
these: "Has
the child been
baptized?"   If
so, "By what
name?" The in-
fant is then reg-
istered on the

THE MOSKWA AND THE KREMLIN.

books of the institution, with a regular number, and a receipt
for it is given to the parents of the infant, who may visit
and even claim the child at any time within ten years.   If I
thought I could make a success of it, I would attempt a
description of what I saw in this vast hospital.   The simple
arts of washing and dressing babies are here brought as near
to perfection as it is possible for me, at least, to imagine.
Suffice it to say, the little foundlings are bathed in copper tubs

lined with thick flannel, and then are dressed on soft pillows,
instead of on the bony knees or sharp crinoline of the nurses.
Yet, notwithstanding these luxuries, at the time of my visit
most of the infants cried more unmusically than I ever heard
babies cry before; but   perhaps it was because they screamed   in Russian.

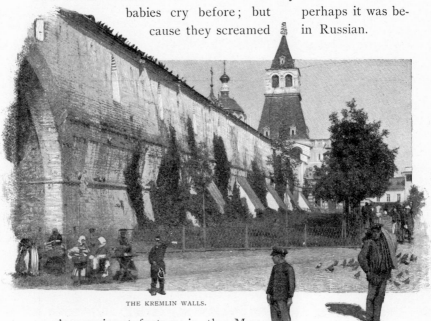

THE KREMLIN WALLS.

A prominent feature in the Mus-
covite capital is the river Moskwa,   which gives the
name "Moscow" to the city through which it flows. If the
tourist should stand on one of the Kremlin towers, one hundred feet above this stream, he would perceive that Moscow
lies in the form of two great circles, — one within the other,
like the rings of a tree. Both represent successive periods
of Moscow's growth. Both are enclosed by walls of fortifi-
cation; and the inner circle, or core, of the Tsar's capital is
its far-famed Kremlin. Before I visited Russia I did not
fully understand what this Kremlin was. In reality it is the
Acropolis of Moscow — a kind of fortress similar to those
built by the Mogul conquerors of India at Agra and at Delhi.

Within its walls are situated the Imperial Palace, the Treasury, the Arsenal, and the most sacred temples in the empire ;
and these, with their gilded domes and variously colored
roofs and walls, display above the Kremlin battlements a
veritable galaxy of splendor.

Before examining these treasures, I carefully observed
the casket that contains them. Originally, the Kremlin was
surrounded by stout walls of oak. More than five hundred
years ago, however, the wooden walls gave place to those
of stone, in order that the Tartars might be more successfully resisted. Again and again, under successive shocks of
war, these battlements have been injured and rebuilt ; but in
their form they have remained substan-   tially the same.
Outlying Moscow was, as all know,   burned by the
Russians to resist Napoleon, yet most   of the Kremlin
fortunately remained unharmed, for the   devouring element did little save to lick the historic   towers with its
tongues of flame. I had imagined this   great Muscovite
citadel blackened by time, or at least   clothed in the
sombre tints that
seem the fitting

A CORNER OF THE KREMLIN.

garb of venerable monuments. Here, however, I was pleas-
antly disappointed. The Russians, like the people of almost
every new nation, love brilliant, striking coloring, and, therefore, they repaint the walls of the Kremlin as often as their
colors fade under the keen breath of the frosty North.

Eager to enter the enclosure of the Kremlin, we made
our way toward its principal entrance. To reach this we
were obliged to cross the famous "Red Square," which
flanks the Kremlin's deeply tinted walls. Its history proves
it to have been well named; for, if its pavement could bear
witness to the dreadful deeds enacted here, it would be red
with blood. Two hundred years ago, this was the place of
public punishment, and in those days of horrible brutality
the victims of despotic cruelty were (as the judges decided)
hanged, broken on the wheel, impaled, beaten to death,
buried alive, or burned in iron cages. Counterfeiters were
stretched on the ground, and molten lead was poured down
their throats, while those who had been guilty of sacrilege
were torn to pieces by iron hooks.

At one extremity of the Red Square stands the world-
renowned Church of St. Basil. The man for whom this

THE RED SQUARE.

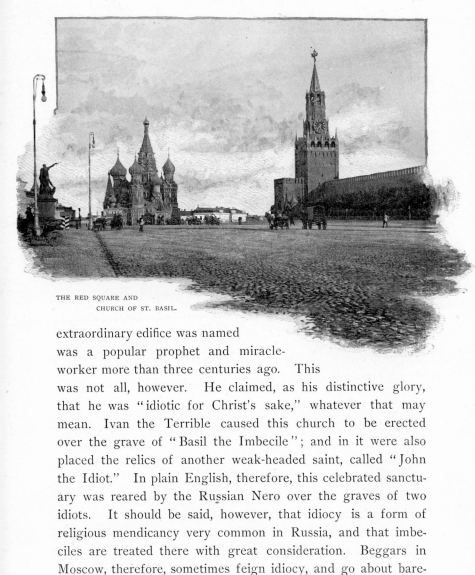

THE RED SQUARE AND
    CHURCH OF ST. BASIL.

extraordinary edifice was named
was a popular prophet and miracle-
worker more than three centuries ago.   This
was not all, however.   He claimed, as his distinctive glory,
that he was "idiotic for Christ's sake," whatever that may
mean.   Ivan the Terrible caused this church to be erected
over the grave of "Basil the Imbecile"; and in it were also
placed the relics of another weak-headed saint, called "John
the Idiot."   In plain English, therefore, this celebrated sanctuary was reared by the Russian Nero over the graves of two
idiots.   It should be said, however, that idiocy is a form of
religious mendicancy very common in Russia, and that imbe-
ciles are treated there with great consideration.   Beggars in
Moscow, therefore, sometimes feign idiocy, and go about bare-
footed in winter; but very few of these are either saints, or
followers of Father Kneipp.

In the crypt of this church are kept the heavy chain and

crosses which St. Basil wore for penance, and the iron
weights worn by the other idiot; but Basil's cap was
carried away by the French in 1812, and the inesti-
mable treasure has never been recovered.

The architecture of this marvelous structure is in-
coherent and amazing, yet, in a certain sense, beautiful. One would, however, never
suspect St. Basil's to be a Christian Church, if it were not for
the gilded

THE CHURCH OF ST. BASIL.

crosses that adorn its towers. The especial glory of the
building is its coloring, the effect of which can hardly be
exaggerated; for it is painted in all the colors of the rain-
bow. Red, orange, yellow, green, blue, violet, gold, and silver
are blended in one amazing mass, like a fantastic castle made
of prisms. From the roof rise eleven towers, apparently
bound together like an immense bouquet of architectural
flowers. Each cupola is different. One represents an arti-

choke, another a pineapple, a third a melon, while others suggest the turbans of Oriental giants. Under each of these is a tiny chapel, from which we looked up at the roof, as from the bottom of a well, only to find in the ceiling a huge mosaic eye, startling us by the vivid scrutiny with which it seemed to regard us.

I admit that this church is strange, fantastic, and to many even displeasing from its very oddity; but to me it seemed precisely suited to the half-barbaric Muscovite capital, and I surveyed it with a singular feeling of satisfaction. If St. Basil's is attractive in summer, how beautiful must it appear in winter time! For then the rays of the sun not only gleam upon its wealth of colors, but likewise sparkle on the towers with their silver frosting, the windows with their diamond pendants, and all its countless ornaments and crosses, set in a mass of glittering crystals, cut by the unrivaled lapidaries of the frosty air. Some one has said that Russia without snow is like an orchard without fruit.

Close by St. Basil's is the most revered of the five portals that pierce the Kremlin walls. It

THE REDEEMER GATE.

is known as the "Redeemer Gate," because above its entrance
is a picture of Christ which is deemed so sacred that no
one is allowed to pass beneath it without removing his hat.
Even the Emperor does not fail to conform to this
custom, whenever he rides into the Kremlin. I have frequently stood here, half an hour at a time, watching
the motley throng of passing Rus- sians; but whether the
travelers were on foot, in drosh- kies, or on horseback, they never failed to uncover their
heads as they crossed the threshold.
When- ever we passed through this por-

THE REDEEMER GATE AND CONVENT.

tal, our guide would always give us the solemn
warning, "Hats off, gentlemen!" Formerly, an omission to
uncover the head here was severely punished; and even
now it would not be advisable to refuse to comply with
the custom. The wise traveler, however, is always cos-
mopolitan enough to obligingly remove his shoes at the

door of a Turkish Mosque, or
his hat at a " Redeemer Gate."

Near this portal is the
Arsenal of the Kremlin,
and most of the eight
hundred and fifty
cannon which it
contains were cap-
tured from the French,
in 1812, and are preserved
as souvenirs of their disastrous
campaign. At one corner of the
building is an enormous cannon.

THE GREAT GUN.

A man can easily stand
beneath it, and the monster's throat is three feet
in diameter. This huge gun has, however, never
been discharged, and it seems to
have been intended for ornament,
not for use.

The most prominent of the
Kremlin structures is
the Ivan Tower. This
is an imposing
and beautiful
monument, for its
octagonal walls
are of snowy
whiteness, and
at a height of
three hundred
and twenty-five
feet it wears a
crown of gold.
For three centuries
this has been the

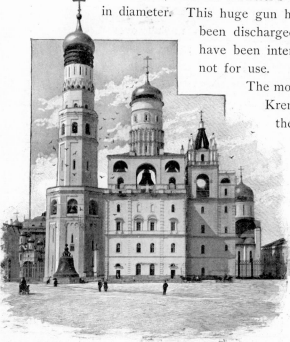

THE IVAN TOWER.

Campanile of the Kremlin. It contains, in fact, no less than thirty-six bells, two of which are of silver, while the largest weighs one hundred and thirty thousand pounds. The mellow, sweet vibrations of a musical bell are among the most agreeable sounds whose waves can fall upon the human ear. There are those who prefer them to all other kinds of music.

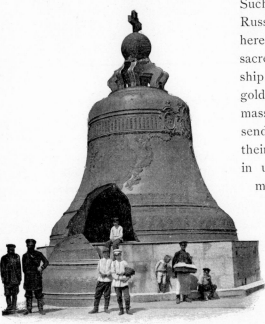

THE KING OF BELLS.

Such persons should come to Russia to be satisfied, for here bells are regarded as sacred instruments of worship; and so much silver and gold are cast into their molten mass that, when finished, they send forth liquid tones from their lofty cages, which roll in unison over the city in majestic harmony like the waves of the sea, or ring out singly in soft, silvery resonance like the song of a bird.

But if the bells within this gold-capped tower amazed us, what could we say when we beheld the monster lying at its base? This is, indeed, the "King of Bells." It looked to me, as I approached it, like a huge bronze tent. Through the aperture in its side, a man can enter without lowering his head, and in the interior there is room for forty people at one time. It has been used as a chapel. It is needless to say that this bell was intended to adorn the belfry of the Ivan Tower, from which, however, it has been forever excluded; for, owing to an imperfection in its casting, a piece weighing

IBERIAN CHAPEL AND RESURRECTION GATE.

eleven tons was broken out of its side, and the bell was ruined. Hence, throughout all the joys and sorrows of the city's history, this " King of Bells" has remained silent since its birth. It must be said, however, that it has filled the world with its renown. As for the broken piece of metal, the peasants claim that a good bell could be made from that alone, as Eve was made out of a rib of Adam.

THE CHURCH OF THE ANNUNCIATION.

While standing in the belfry of the Ivan Tower, I watched with interest the immense flocks of pigeons which sometimes came in clouds about the buildings. In fact, pigeons are more numerous in Moscow than in Venice, for to a Russian the dove is a sacred bird, — a living emblem of the Holy Spirit.

From this aërial bell-tower one looks directly down upon the most sacred edifice in Russia — the Cathedral of the Assumption. It is severely plain in appearance, and its whitewashed walls give no hint of the treasures contained

THE PALACE AND THE MOSKWA.

beneath its gilded domes. But in reality gigantic gilded columns support its roof, and sacred pictures line its walls from floor to ceiling like a tapestry of gold.

It is in this cathedral that, amid the most imposing ceremonies, all the Tsars, from Ivan the Terrible to the present sovereign, have been crowned. To speak more exactly, however, they have crowned themselves; for no one is deemed worthy, at that solemn hour, to place upon the Emperor's brow the emblem of sovereignty, save the Tsar himself. We beheld the very platform on which they have all, in succession, stood.

Leaving the cathedral, a few steps brought us to the famous Palace of the Kremlin, which contains some of the richest and most elegant

ST. GEORGE'S HALL.

HOLY GATE OF KREMLIN.

apartments I have ever seen. In the Hall of St. George, for example, columns of alabaster support a gilded roof, from which descend magnificent chandeliers; while on the walls gilded letters spell the names of all the heroes who have been decorated with St. George's cross, — the highest military order in the empire. This room, however, honors the illustrious living as well as the distinguished dead; for it is here that, on State occasions, the Emperor receives foreign ambassadors and royal guests.

ST. ANDREW'S HALL.

At right angles to the Hall of St. George, is another magnificent apartment, known as the Hall of St. Andrew. Here twisted pillars, enriched with flowers of gold, rise on every side, while fourteen lofty mirrors reflect as many windows, opening upon the balconies of the Kremlin. The inlaid floor is wonderfully designed, every kind of wood being used to produce intricate and elaborate patterns of scrolls and flowers; its gorgeous ceiling, sparkling with gilding and heraldic devices, glitters sixty-eight feet above the pavement; and the walls, which are hung in light pink silk and gold, form beautiful expanses of marble, golden ornamentation, and paintings. At one extremity of the room are two black velvet stands, on which are placed rare gold and silver ornaments of the imperial family when the Emperor is residing here. Passing between these, and beneath the richly decorated portal, I found myself before the throne of the Tsar.

It is a seat worthy of an imperial potentate. The wall behind it is of light blue silk. The steps which lead to it are of marble. Beautiful curtains hang on either side. The framework is a mass of gold, encrusted with rare gems,

THE TSAR'S THRONE.

and on the summit of the splendid canopy is a golden crown. Within, is the richly gilded chair, outlined against a background of red velvet, in which are wrought, in precious stones, the double-headed eagles of the empire. Yet, notwithstanding all this splendor, I recollected the words of Napoleon: "What is a throne, a few boards covered with gold and velvet? No, the real throne is the man."

THE TREASURY.

A MOSCOW STREET SCENE.

Words are almost powerless to describe the Treasury of
the Kremlin; for it contains so marvelous a collection of
historic relics and souvenirs of conquest that it would be
folly to attempt to enumerate them. In fact, from her
connection with Asia, Persia, and India, Russia has had
unusual opportunities to secure a multitude of precious
objects; and, cer-
tainly, with the
exception of the
Sultan's Treasury
at Constantinople,
I have never seen
such a display as
this. Here are
preserved the
coronation robes
of many of the
Empresses, and
the jewels and
insignia of former
Tsars. As we
walked along
these glittering

A CORRIDOR IN THE KREMLIN PALACE.

corridors, we saw at every turn crowns radiant with resplendent
colors, and sceptres scintillating waves of brilliancy. If this
statement seems extravagant, remember that one of these sceptres contains no less than two hundred and eighty-six diamonds
and three hundred and sixty rubies. Here also is a throne from
Persia, still sparkling with three thousand precious stones; and
under a protecting canopy of velvet and gold is the magnificent imperial chair, upon which sat as joint sovereigns of
Russia the two brothers, one of whom was destined soon to
rule alone under the well-earned title of Peter the Great.

I observed with interest, also, the elegant canopy under

which every Tsar walks in solemn procession to and from his
coronation, and a chair containing, it is said, a piece of
the true Cross.   Here, too, in striking contrast to this dazzling
wealth, I saw the simple camp bedstead of Napoleon, captured by the Russians during the retreat of the French
across the Beresina.

Aside from the memories of Russian sovereigns, evoked
by this old palace, another epoch in its history was
continually present, reminding me that less than a century ago a foreign sovereign and conqueror walked through
these halls, and for a time resided here, sending meantime
decrees and orders to his own capital, two thousand miles
away; among them being the rules which, to-day, still govern the Comédie Française at Paris.   There was something
sublime in the way in which the Russians here opposed the
hitherto invincible Napoleon.   To thwart him, they gave to
the devouring element their ancient, beautiful, and holy city,
although it was the idol of every Russian heart, and though
her shrines were to them the holiest in the world, hallowed
by centuries of historical association.   This fearful sea of flame
spoke, therefore, in a million fiery tongues of the grandest
sacrifice ever made to national feeling, and threw a lurid glare
on the descending path that ended in the lonely grave at St.
Helena.

THE BURNING OF MOSCOW.